Praise for *The Warehouse*

"If you've been searching for an accessible introduction to mass criminalization in the US, look no further than *The Warehouse*. This book is visually captivating and full of valuable information for youth and adults alike. I'll be gifting this book to people for years to come and will recommend it to everyone who asks me the question: 'What is mass incarceration?'"

—Mariame Kaba, author of *We Do This 'til We Free Us:*
Abolitionist Organizing and Transforming Justice

"This book vividly activates the senses in its sharp, accessible, and principled analysis of the scope and scale of the carceral state. From cops to cages, from 'get tough' politics to the economics of phone calls, e-carceration, and rural prison building, and from incremental legislative reforms to the visionary organizing of abolitionists, Kilgore and Liu break down the contours of this warehouse and illuminate our paths toward dismantling it."

—Judah Schept, author of *Coal, Cages, Crisis:*
The Rise of the Prison Economy in Central Appalachia

"An essential resource for classroom teaching and movement building from someone on the front lines of the battle to dismantle the prison-industrial complex."

—Alex S. Vitale, author of *The End of Policing*

"A visually stunning primer on how the US became the world's incarceration nation. Read it and learn how the criminal punishment system works, whom it affects, and what we, as a society, could be doing instead."

—Victoria Law, author of *"Prisons Make Us Safer":*
And 20 Other Myths about Mass Incarceration

"Through crystal-clear prose and striking illustrations, *The Warehouse* maps the jagged landscape of mass incarceration, leaving the reader both utterly convinced of the system's injustice and keenly equipped to help dismantle it. *The Warehouse* manages to be both sweeping in scope and eminently practical: an essential primer for organizers, scholars, journalists, students, and anyone who dreams of an end to oppressive systems. Next time someone asks me to explain incarceration, I will simply hand them this brilliant book!"

—Maya Schenwar, coauthor of *Prison by Any Other Name*

T0384415

"A smartly crafted, beautifully illustrated guide to the violence of human caging. Kilgore and Liu have created a compelling illustration of the many horrors of mass incarceration. What's more, it shows us what change looks like. *The Warehouse* is a vital primer on the cruelty of American prisons and the promise of a world more just that begins when we imagine otherwise."

—Dan Berger, author of *Stayed on Freedom:*
The Long History of Black Power through One Family's Journey

"This is the resource organizers working with communities to end mass incarceration and the expanding police state have been looking for. From seasoned veterans to those looking for an introduction into the subject, this book breaks down the historical, political, social, and economic motives behind the literal and figurative warehousing of millions of human beings in digestible and deeply impactful language and imagery. A must-have for every organizer's toolbelt."

—Hiram Rivera, founder and executive director at
Community Resource Hub for Safety & Accountability

"James Kilgore is one of my favorite commentators regarding the phenomenon of mass incarceration and the necessity of pursuing truly transformative change."

—Michelle Alexander, author of *The New Jim Crow*

"James Kilgore and Vic Liu have given us an essential resource on the multiple, intertwined structures of violence that congeal in mass incarceration—from prisons, jails, and youth and migrant detention centers to solitary confinement, gender-based and sexual violence, and aging in cages to parole, probation, e-carceration, and the perils of reentry. *The Warehouse* braids together deeply researched analysis with crisp, powerful visualizations of data, as well as testimonies and illustrations created by formerly and currently incarcerated peoples, both tender and fierce. Crucially, Kilgore and Liu focus not only on the problem of US imprisonment, but on the resistance and innovation of the people most directly affected by it, including the artwork featured in its pages. By reflecting on movements and campaigns, they point us toward the pitfalls of reform and the horizon of abolition."

—A. Naomi Paik, author of *Bans, Walls, Raids, Sanctuary:*
Understanding U.S. Immigration for the 21st Century

"*The Warehouse* skillfully paints a comprehensive picture of the prison system in a way that is easy to understand, visually stunning, and centers the humanity of incarcerated people. Kilgore and Liu have combine their skills to create a powerful resource for fighting and ending incarceration."

—Sheila Nezhad, development director of Interrupting Criminalization

THE WAREHOUSE

A Visual Primer on Mass Incarceration

JAMES KILGORE
AND VIC LIU

The Warehouse: A Visual Primer on Mass Incarceration
© 2024 James Kilgore and Vic Liu
This edition © 2024 PM Press

Illustrations on pp. 140, 141, and 143 reprinted with permission from Angelo, *Prisoners' Inventions*, Half Letter Press, 2001 (expanded edition, 2020).

ISBN: 979-8-88744-042-2 (paperback)
ISBN: 979-8-88744-052-1 (ebook)
Library of Congress Control Number: 2023944314
Cover illustration and design by Vic Liu
Interior design by Vic Liu

10 9 8 7 6 5 4 3 2 1

PM Press
PO Box 23912
Oakland, CA 94623
www.pmpress.org

Printed in the USA.

Contents

1   Part 1: The Big Picture

39   Part 2: Journey through Incarceration

Jail and Sentencing

Life in Prison

Release

Marginalized in Prison

Resistance

157   Part 3: Dismantling the System and Building Anew

182   Notes

191   Acknowledgments

"All over the world, the institution of the prison serves as a place to **warehouse** people who represent major social problems. ... Prison serves as an institution that consolidates the state's inability and refusal to address the most pressing social problems of this era."

ANGELA DAVIS

Freedom Is a Constant Struggle

PART 1
THE BIG PICTURE

The US has built the largest system of incarceration in human history.

The US incarcerates more people than any other country, incarcerating roughly 20% of the entire global prison population. By contrast, the US population is only 4% of the global population. The US incarcerates 5 times more people than proportionate to its population.

As of 2022, this system held 1.9 million people in a total of 1,833 state prisons, 110 federal prisons, 1,772 juvenile detention facilities, 3,134 local jails, 218 immigration detention facilities, and 80 Indian Country jails. By comparison, in 1980 the combined prison and jail population was just over 500,000.[1]

Who Are the Incarcerated?

The burden of incarceration does not hit the entire population evenly. Overall, people from low-income families are the most likely to be incarcerated. But even within that population, there are serious racial differences. Overall, Black people are far more likely than anyone else to be incarcerated.

People of Color

In 2019, Black people were incarcerated at the rate of 1,240 per 100,000. The rate for Latinx people was 349, for white people 261. However, the rate for Latinx people was artificially low, because many prison and jail systems classify some Latinx people as white. For the same reason, the official white incarceration rate is artificially high.[2]

Wisconsin has the highest incarceration rate of Black people. One Black person out of 36 is behind bars in Wisconsin, as compared to 1 Black person in 214 in Massachusetts. In 7 states, Black people are at least 9 times more likely to be incarcerated than whites (California, Connecticut, Iowa, Maine, Minnesota, New Jersey, Wisconsin).

COMPARED TO WHITE PEOPLE,

BLACK PEOPLE ARE 5X MORE LIKELY
TO BE INCARCERATED.

NATIVE PEOPLE ARE 3X MORE LIKELY
TO BE INCARCERATED.

LATINX PEOPLE ARE 2X MORE LIKELY
TO BE INCARCERATED.

Between 1980 and 2019, the population incarcerated in women's facilities grew by more than 7x.

LGBTQ+ People

LGBTQ+ people are also disproportionately incarcerated. Though the criminal legal system does not keep very accurate data on LGBTQ+ folks, one study estimated that there were 4,890 transgender people living in state prisons across the US. Typically these individuals are housed according to the sex assigned them at birth, not according to their lived gender. Out of those 4,890 transgender people, the study could only confirm 15 cases where people were housed according to their lived gender. LGBTQ+ folks are incarcerated at 3 times the rate of cisgender people.[3]

Nearly 2 in 5 people in prison have at least 1 disability.[4]

Population of Women's Prisons

The burdens of mass incarceration are apportioned according to gender as well as race. While the vast majority of people in prisons and jails are in men's facilities (about 93%), the populations of women's prisons have grown faster than men's facilities.

Although people who identify as women are incarcerated at a lower rate, the absence of men in households and communities shifts a host of tasks onto the folks who are left behind—in the majority of instances, this means mothers, sisters, spouses, girlfriends, or grandmothers who take on increased responsibility for financial and emotional support for the family, childcare, and driving and car maintenance, as well as having to provide financial and emotional support to the person who is incarcerated.

LGBTQ+ people are incarcerated at a rate 3x higher than the general adult population.[6]

People with Disabilities

People categorized as disabled are disproportionately incarcerated. For example, nearly 4 in 10 individuals in state prisons and 3 in 10 in the federal system are listed as having a disability. The Bureau of Justice Statistics reports that fully 1 in 5 people in prison have a serious mental illness. A quarter of individuals incarcerated in state prisons reported having a cognitive disability; 12% have an ambulatory disability, 10% a hearing disability, and 12% are visually challenged. Yet most prisons and jails offer few, if any, accommodations for people with disabilities. Even basic services like sign language interpretation, tables with wheelchair access, hearing aids, and books that are accessible for blind people are more often than not absent.[5]

In 1972, less than 338,000 people were incarcerated in the United States.

Each silhouette represents 1,000 people incarcerated in the US.

By 2021, more than 1,774,000 people were incarcerated in the United States.

Why the Prison Boom?

This boom of incarceration began to spike in the 1980s and continued uninterrupted until 2010, when it began a slow decline. Many factors contributed to this enormous expansion. The boom varied geographically, but during that period every single state experienced a significant growth in its prison and jail population.

The most important reason behind the prison boom was a change in the philosophy of how to solve social problems. Sparked by a resurgence in racism during the 1970s, federal, state, and local governments turned to incarceration and policing to solve social problems like housing shortages, substance use issues, unemployment, immigration, and family conflict. Once the boom took off, those who benefited from this expansion continued to press for more prisons. This included police, prison staff, and elected officials who voted to build prisons to provide jobs for their constituencies. In addition, many businesses benefited from prison expansion, including architectural firms and construction companies that won contracts to build new facilities.

In 1984, there were 903 state prisons. By 1990, that number had risen to 1,207, an increase of 34%. California led the increase in new prison builds, growing from 30 prisons in 1984 to 100 in 1990. These cost the taxpayer dearly. According to a study by the Office of the Inspector General, the federal government built 13 new prisons between 1985 and 2000 at an average cost of $121 million each. At the same time, according to a Sentencing Project report, during the 1990s crime was falling. From 1991 to 1998, violent crime fell by 25% and crime overall declined by 22%. Yet the construction of prisons and jails continued. By 2021, the US had more than 1,500 state prisons, over 2,800 local jails, plus 1,510 juvenile correctional facilities, 186 immigration prisons, 102 federal prisons, and 82 Indian Country jails.[7]

A 2017 report by the Prison Policy Initiative estimated the cost of mass incarceration at $182 billion, with $80.7 billion going to prisons, jails, probation, and parole.[8]

1968   1970   1972   1974   1976   1978   1980   1982   1984   1986   1988   1990   19

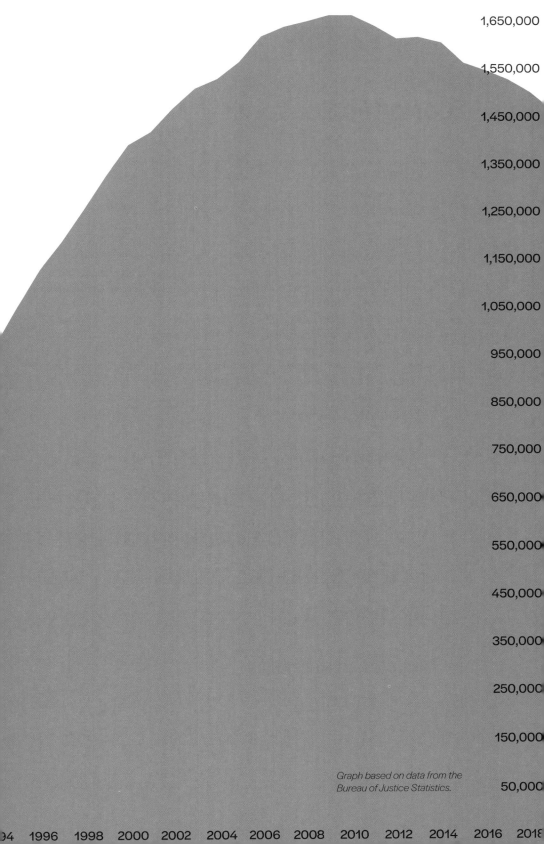

1,650,000

1,550,000

1,450,000

1,350,000

1,250,000

1,150,000

1,050,000

950,000

850,000

750,000

650,000

550,000

450,000

350,000

250,000

150,000

Graph based on data from the
Bureau of Justice Statistics.   50,000

94   1996   1998   2000   2002   2004   2006   2008   2010   2012   2014   2016   2018

Economic Reasons

In her renowned book *Golden Gulag*, Ruth Wilson Gilmore linked the rise of mass incarceration to economic crisis. She argued that falling corporate profit rates prompted the US government to reduce corporate taxes. The falling tax levels meant less revenue for the government, which then triggered reductions in government spending on social services like food stamps (now called the Supplemental Nutrition Assistance Program, or SNAP), public housing, and other forms of social welfare. As the crime levels rose, budgets for social services shifted into law enforcement, including prison and jail construction. Many elected officials also joined in the call for tough-on-crime measures, ways to "lock 'em up and throw away the key."

Moreover, once prison and jail building began to expand, the carceral system built up an economic following of its own—hundreds of thousands of individuals who depended on it for their livelihood. Police and prison guards' unions, such as the Police Benevolent Association of New York and the California Correctional and Police Officers Association (CCPOA), began to flex their financial muscle by making large donations to the electoral campaigns of candidates who supported prison building.

"Doubling the conviction rate in this country would do more to cure crime in America than quadrupling the funds for…war on poverty."[9]

PRESIDENT RICHARD NIXON

Groundbreaking of Prison in Stanislaus County
One of the newest prison projects in California begins as mass incarceration continues to expand. Note the green tarp to protect their shoes for the photoshoot.
Marshall Project, courtesy of Stanislaus County

In the late 1960s and 1970s, there
were a few major recessions.

Corporate profits fell.

The US government
cut corporate taxes to aid
economic recovery.

The US government received
less tax revenue.

The US government reduced
spending on social services.
These included food stamps (now called
SNAP), public housing, and other forms of
social welfare.

Crime levels rose.

The US built more prisons.
Instead of reincreasing budgets for social
services, governments instead increased
budgets for law enforcement, including prison
and jail construction.

Philosophical Reasons

The rise of mass incarceration coincided with a philosophical shift in analyzing the root causes of crime. The social justice movements of the 1960s and 1970s had framed crime as the result of structural issues, particularly poverty and inequality. In this vein, prisons and supervision were viewed as areas of rehabilitation and personal development. Resources in prisons included education programs and job training.

But in the 1980s, the philosophical pendulum began to swing in the other direction. Crime was viewed as the result of personal flaws and failure. The cure was no longer to provide support and rehabilitation to people but to punish them, to "teach them a lesson" by denying them their freedom.

One of the most powerful indicators of the demise of rehabilitation was the demise of education programs. In 1979, 41% of all people incarcerated in state prisons were enrolled in some type of education. By 1995, the figure had fallen to 22%. Similarly, higher education fell away. In 1993, there were more than 350 college education programs in prisons. Financing for most of the students came via federal Pell Grants. But in 1993, Congress voted to eliminate these grants. As a result, by 2005 there were only a dozen college-in-prison programs still operating.[10]

BEFORE THE 1980S	AFTER THE 1980S
REHABILITATION	**PUNISHMENT**
Crime is believed to be caused by **structural issues, like poverty, racism, and inequality.**	Crime is believed to be caused by **personal flaws and failure.**
Prisons exist to **rehabilitate and foster personal development.**	Prisons exist to **punish or teach people a lesson.**

"Imprisonment has become the response of first resort to far too many of the social problems that burden people who are ensconced in poverty.

These problems often are veiled by being conveniently grouped together under the category 'crime' and by the automatic attribution of criminal behavior to people of color. Homelessness, unemployment, drug addiction, mental illness, and illiteracy are only a few of the problems that disappear from public view when the human beings contending with them are relegated to cages.

Prisons thus perform a feat of magic. Or rather the people who continually vote in new prison bonds and tacitly assent to a proliferating network of prisons and jails have been tricked into believing in the magic of imprisonment. **But prisons do not disappear problems, they disappear human beings.**"[11]

ANGELA DAVIS

Changes in Sentencing

Sentencing depends on how the prosecutor charges the crime, rather than judicial discretion.

One of the most important factors that has sparked the increase in the number of people incarcerated in the US has been the changes in sentencing laws. Before the 1980s, most courts practiced indeterminate sentencing. Under this system, the judge had lots of discretion in deciding a person's fate. For example, in some states the law might specify that a person convicted of selling drugs could receive a sentence of 0 to 15 years. The judge could then sentence the person under the law to anywhere from no prison time to a maximum of 15 years.

Moreover, once a person was sent to prison, they could earn good time. For example, under the federal system before mass incarceration, a person would have to serve $\frac{1}{3}$ of their sentence before becoming eligible for parole. If they had completed that $\frac{1}{3}$ of their sentence, they would go before a parole board, who would decide if they merited release. If they had avoided disciplinary write-ups, maintained a job in the prison, and had a clear-cut plan for parole, they could be released. If they had not shown "good behavior," they would be sent back into the prison and reviewed again a year or two later. Hence there was an incentive for them to follow the prison program.

Mandatory Minimums

Mandatory minimums made the system more punitive. Under mandatory minimums, the judges lost most of their power to determine sentences. Sentences for specific crimes were prescribed with very little leeway for judges to take an individual's life circumstances or background into account. For example, under the federal system, a person convicted of selling 28 grams of cocaine (about 1 ounce) had to be given a minimum of 5 years in prison, regardless of the person's criminal history, personal circumstances, or actual role in the sale. This shifted the power in sentencing from judges to prosecutors. The outcome of an individual's case depended more on what charges were pressed against them than a judge's case-by-case evaluation of a person. And the new sentencing laws made penalties much stiffer, especially in drug-related cases.

HAMEDAH HASAN was 21 years old when she fled her abusive relationship and stayed with her cousin. Her cousin was involved in selling crack cocaine, and she agreed to help him by running some errands and transferring money.

Even though Hamedah was:

pregnant

nonviolent

a survivor of abuse

a single mother of two young daughters

and had a clean record,

because she helped wire money and ran errands for her cousin, she was sentenced to life in prison.

"It is my strongly felt opinion that neither T. Lomax nor S. Lomax ought to spend the rest of their days in prison. However, I have not yet found a principled basis for imposing a lesser sentence under the Guidelines."

RICHARD G. KOPF [12]

the presiding judge, referring to Hamedah by her given name, Stephanie Lomax

The Three Strikes Law

Another key element of harsh sentencing was the three strikes law. Under this legislation, a person who committed three violent felonies (each one called a strike) would face an automatic sentence of life imprisonment without parole. In some states, people were "struck out" for relatively minor offenses. In Washington State, a group of prosecutors sent an open letter to voters in opposition to three strikes laws. They gave this example:

"An 18-year-old high school senior pushes a classmate down to steal his Michael Jordan $150 sneakers—Strike One; he gets out of jail and shoplifts a jacket from the Bon Marche, pushing aside the clerk as he runs out of the store—Strike Two; he gets out of jail, straightens out, and 9 years later gets in a fight in a bar and intentionally hits someone, breaking his nose—criminal behavior, to be sure, but hardly the crime of the century, yet it is Strike Three. He is sent to prison for the rest of his life."[13]

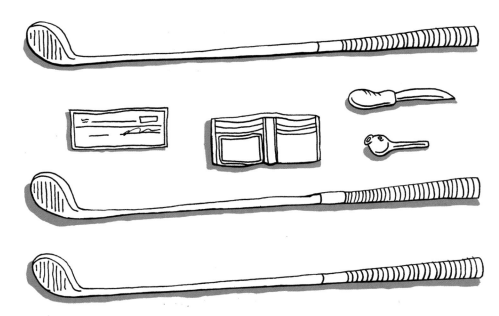

Gary Ewing's Three Strikes
The Supreme Court upheld the decision to sentence Ewing to 25 years to life under the three strikes law for stealing three golf clubs on top of previous felony crimes that included armed robbery.

Truth in Sentencing

In the late 1970s, most states and the federal government moved away from indeterminate sentences to truth in sentencing along with mandatory minimums. Under truth in sentencing, a person could not reduce their sentence through "good behavior." They would receive a sentence for a stipulated period of time and be compelled to serve a designated percentage of that time. For example, they might be given a 10-year sentence at 50%, which would mean 5 years, or that same 10-year sentence at 100%, meaning they would have to serve all 10 years before release regardless of their behavior. The release date would not be set by the parole board but at the time of sentencing.[14]

RACIAL DISPARITY IN SENTENCING CHANGES

According to the Sentencing Project, in 2018, 48% of those serving life or "virtual life" sentences were Black. A "virtual life" sentence is a number of years that exceed the life expectancy of the individual.[15]

Progressive Prosecutors as Pushback

One form of pushback against this was the move to elect progressive prosecutors, individuals who back criminal justice reform and would therefore change the way in which people were charged. Several cities elected progressive prosecutors. Likely the two most well known were Larry Krasner in Philadelphia and Chesa Boudin in San Francisco. Krasner was elected in 2017, Boudin in 2019. Both campaigned on programs targeted at reducing jail populations by reducing drug arrests and ending cash bail. However, both faced massive backlash from police unions and corporate supporters of a law-and-order approach. As a result, both faced legal proceedings against them. Boudin was removed from office via a recall vote in 2022, and Krasner was impeached in the same year for alleged corruption.

Political Reasons

The social movements of the 1960s and 1970s—the Black liberation and civil rights struggles, the antiwar movement, women's and gay liberation movements—created a wave of fear among the white middle-class population, who felt their security and political power was under threat. Politicians like presidents Richard Nixon and Ronald Reagan played on this fear by exaggerating the realities of crime.

In her famous book *The New Jim Crow*, Michelle Alexander spelled out how the advances of the antiracist movements had made it difficult for politicians to promote an overtly racist agenda that explicitly blamed Black people for the wave of crime. Instead, Alexander contended that conservatives used terms like "criminal" and "predator" as a suggestive way of referring to Black people.

These factors were so powerful that every US president from Nixon onward adopted the principles of mass incarceration and punishment.

1969–1974

The Nixon Presidency

President Richard Nixon's 1971 speech is typically categorized as the starting point of the War on Drugs. Despite the fact that at the time the US had over 300,000 troops still fighting in Southeast Asia, Nixon declared drugs as the country's most important enemy. Nixon went on to create the Drug Enforcement Administration (DEA) in 1973. This agency is a special branch of law enforcement

PRESIDENT CALLS FOR 'TOTAL WAR' ON U.S. ADDICTION

...s in City on Drug
...ith Rockefeller
...High Officials

PUSHERS

committed to targeting illegal drug use and smuggling in the United States.

At the start, the DEA was given 1,470 special agents and a budget of less than $75 million. Today, the agency has nearly 5,000 agents and a budget of $2.03 billion.

The War on Drugs also brought harsher sentencing laws. Most notorious was mandatory minimums, which set fixed penalties for specific crimes, giving judges little or no leeway to adjust the sentence depending on a person's circumstances or family responsibilities.[16]

Ulterior Motives behind the War on Drugs?

In a 1994 interview, Nixon's domestic policy chief, John Erhlichman, explained that the Nixon campaign had two enemies: the antiwar left and Black people. "We knew we couldn't make it illegal to be either against the war or Black, but by getting the public to associate the hippies with marijuana and Blacks with heroin, and then criminalizing both heavily, we could disrupt those communities. We could arrest their leaders, raid their homes, break up their meetings, and vilify them night after night on the evening news. Did we know we were lying about the drugs? Of course we did."

When Nixon resigned from the presidency in 1973, the War on Drugs lost momentum. But it didn't die.

1981–1989

The Reagan Presidency

Ronald Reagan reiterated Nixon's mantra, labeling drugs as the number one public enemy in the US, despite the fact that Gallup polls showed only 2% of the population categorized drugs as the top domestic issue.[17]

Along with his wife, Nancy Reagan, he launched the "Just Say No" campaign. The first lady made more than 250 public appearances, often meeting with school pupils and sympathetic members of the public and urging them to "Just Say No" to drugs. Over 10,000 Just Say No clubs were established in schools. Michael Jackson joined the effort, creating a song about drugs to the tune of his hit "Beat It."

LA police chief Daryl Gates, who argued that "casual drug users should be taken out and shot," founded the Drug Abuse Resistance Education program (DARE), which encouraged children to inform the police if they knew of anyone who used drugs, including their own parents. According to DARE, the three Rs meant "Recognize, Resist, and Report."

With the War on Drugs came the militarization of the police—the foot soldiers in the battle. Across the country, special weapons and tactical teams emerged. Police armed themselves with automatic weapons, tanks, and helicopters. Prison populations soared from 330,000 in 1980 to over 603,000 by the end of Reagan's presidency.

The War on Drugs was the key laboratory for applying mandatory minimum sentences. Perhaps the most notorious sentencing measure was the 1986 Anti-Drug Abuse Act, which put in place harsh mandatory minimums for drug offenses. The most notorious of these penalties was the racist policy in regard to cocaine. The penalties for an ounce of crack cocaine, largely used by Black people, was the same as the penalty for 100 ounces of powder cocaine, more frequently used by white people. The late Black commentator Glen Ford described this as a model "of efficiency in the destruction of the Black lives." These inequities would only be reduced (not eliminated) in 2011.

"I now have absolute proof that smoking even one marijuana cigarette is equal in brain damage to being on Bikini Island during an H-bomb blast."[18]

RONALD REAGAN

1986   1987

BRING BACK THE DEATH PENALTY
BRING BACK POLICE!

Willie Horton

White House Set Up Drug Buy in the Park For Bush TV Spee

By MAUREEN DOWD
Special to The New York Times
KENNEBUNKPORT, Me., Sept. 2
— Government agents lured a drug

The Bush Sr. Presidency

In George H.W. Bush's first presidential address from the Oval Office in 1989, he held up a bag of what he said was "innocent looking as candy, but it's turning our cities into battle zones." It was rocks of crack cocaine that he claimed had been seized during an arrest in Lafayette Park, which is adjacent to the White House. He called drugs "the greatest domestic threat facing our nation today."

Though drug use had declined by the time Bush Senior came into office, he amped up the War on Drugs again, spending $45 billion to reinvigorate drug law enforcement, more than the previous 4 presidents combined. His actions included the 1033 program, which delivered military vehicles and hardware to local police departments.

Bush Senior also internationalized the War on Drugs, moving the US military in to fight drug lords in Colombia, Bolivia, and Peru. By the end of his presidency, the Pentagon's counternarcotics budget had increased by over 100,000%. And the population in prisons in the US had risen from 631,990 in 1988 to 888,593 in 1992. This was an overall increase of 182% over the figure at the outset of the Reagan administration in 1980.

The Clinton Presidency

The 1986 Anti-Drug Abuse Bill and the enormous expansion of prison populations had done little to reduce crime rates by the time Bill Clinton took office in 1992. Bipartisan support was mounting for yet another round of punitive legislation. Democrats like Senator Joe Biden and Republicans like Strom Thurmond were walking hand in hand when it came to expanding the power of police and building more prisons. Even a significant cohort of Black political leaders backed the bill, including the majority of the Congressional Black Caucus. Bill Clinton rode this bipartisan anticrime wave and became the champion of "lock 'em up and throw away the key." In his words, "Gangs and drugs have taken over our streets and undermined our schools."

This enthusiasm for punishment combined with budgetary allocations sparked the greatest expansion of prisons in US history. **From 1990 to 2005, the number of prisons rose by 43%.** The prison population expanded during Clinton's years in office from just under 900,000 to more than 1.3 million. Racialized drug prosecutions fueled much of this. From 1991 to 2001, 9 times as many Black people as white people went to federal prison for crack offenses. Black people's sentences for crack were double that for white crack offenders in federal court during that period: 148 months compared to 84 months.

The 1994 Crime Act

Officially known as the Violent Crime Control and Law Enforcement Act of 1994, the 1994 Crime Act was likely the most far-reaching punitive bill of the era of mass incarceration. It included $12.5 billion for new state prisons. To receive a portion of these funds, a state government had to pass harsh truth-in-sentencing laws. The bill also authorized the death penalty for 60 new federal offenses and imposed mandatory life sentences for people with three or more felonies of a certain type. In addition, harsher penalties were applied to youth who broke the law, the group the president's wife, Hillary, had referred to as "super predators." Historian Elizabeth Hinton argued that President Clinton's law-and-order campaign was done with full awareness of the racial implications. She wrote that "The Clinton administration knew that the criminal justice system was deeply unfair and biased against African Americans, and chose to expand that system."

After the Republicans seized control of Congress in the historic 1994 midterm elections, the Clinton White House sought to double down on its law-and-order image in advance of the 1996 presidential race. In the short term, it was a winning political strategy for Clinton. In the long term, it would help pave the way to one of the worst laws of his presidency.

Increase in Immigration Criminalization

Clinton's law-and-order crusade did not stop at the criminal legal system. Under his watch, repression of immigrants also heightened. The Illegal Immigration Reform and Immigrant Responsibility Act of 1996 put in place the administrative machinery to step up deportation and reduce the pathways for immigrants to attain citizenship. It also made anyone with a felony conviction subject to deportation, even if the felony occurred before the bill was passed. Deportations escalated. From 1992 to 2000, deportations to Mexico more than quadrupled.

As the century drew to a close, the United States was cementing itself in the position of the world's largest incarcerator, with Black people being the primary targets of this systematic repression. But while the prison population was steadily rising, crime levels showed contradictory patterns. According to the Brennan Center think tank, crime hit an all-time high in 1991 and then began a general decline. However, while all states increased their prison populations during this

1995   1996

period, the impact on crime varied. In cities such as New York and Portland, Oregon, the overall crime rate, the murder rate, and the violent crime rate fell dramatically from 1990 to 2010. By contrast, Philadelphia had a fluctuating incidence of murder and violent crime during that period.

"Unless we do something about that cadre of young people —tens of thousands of them born out of wedlock, without parents, without supervision, without any structure, without any conscience developing ... they will ... become the predators 15 years from now."

JOE BIDEN
senator from Delaware at the time, 1993

2001–2009

The George W. Bush Presidency

George W. Bush continued the War on Drugs but shifted targets from his predecessors. He prioritized attacking the use of marijuana. By 2005, arrests for marijuana accounted for almost half of the nation's drug busts, almost double the amount a decade earlier. Across the country, drug enforcement teams mounted raids on medical marijuana dispensaries. As of 2022, at least 13 states were requiring drug testing for recipients of public benefits.

Like his father, he also kept an international focus on the war, spending $5.4 billion during his first term to eradicate cocaine production and trafficking from Latin America. The result: coca cultivation in the Andes of South America rose 29%.

Yet after the 9/11 attacks on the World Trade Center in 2001, the focus on drugs drifted. As the FBI stated at the time, "The number-one stated priority for the FBI is to prevent another attack. ... Other things are not the primary focus. We've had to retool."

"The president could sell the War on Drugs in peacetime but ... to continue that kind of rhetoric in the middle of a real war, when American soldiers are getting blown up in Iraq, makes it look trivial."[19]

TIMOTHY LYNCH
director of the Project on Criminal Justice at the conservative Cato Institute

2004   2005   2006   2007   2008

2009–2017

The Obama Presidency

Obama came to the presidency with a quiet determination to fundamentally alter the War on Drugs. To begin with, he stopped using that term, preferring, in the media at least, to cast drugs as a public health issue. He undertook three major steps of reform. For the first time since the days of Jimmy Carter, the federal budget allocated more money to drug treatment than drug law enforcement. Moreover, as a number of states stepped up efforts to legalize or decriminalize marijuana, Obama didn't use the existing federal law, which still outlawed cannabis, to overrule the states. Lastly, he did grant release to a number of people in the federal prison system who had received long sentences for low-level drug offenses. As a result, the federal prison system population actually fell during the Obama years for the first time in decades.

The 21st Century Cures Act

Furthermore, the opioid epidemic surfaced during Obama's second term. Rather than the "lock 'em up and throw away the key" approach that had dominated the early years of the drug war, the administration's response was a public health initiative, the 21st Century Cures Act, which added $6.3 billion to public health spending on opioid addiction treatment.

2010   2011   2012

While these high-profile actions slowed down the drug war offensive, the shape of mass incarceration and the paradigm of punishment did not fundamentally change. Some observers referred to the Cures Act as "lipstick on a pig," as it added funding to opioid treatment by slashing funds from other public health initiatives such as immunizations and tobacco consumption. Moreover, the response to the opioid epidemic, which directly impacted white people from reasonably well-to-do families, sparked a different policy and media response than the crusades of the 1980s and 1990s, which depicted Black drug users as "crackheads" and their children as "crack babies." The policy and media response was typically: How can we punish these people and keep them off the streets? Media often portrayed white opioid users sympathetically; it highlighted their success stories and labeled their addiction as tragedy rather than degeneracy. Black baseball star Darryl Strawberry, whose challenges with substance use became a media story, noted that "the stigma was so wrong for African Americans. They couldn't get the help they needed because everybody looked at them as 'less than.'"

Obama's efforts to address the racialized disparities between punishment for crack and powder cocaine reduced but did not eliminate the inequality, leaving the same punishment in place for 1 ounce of crack cocaine as for 18 ounces of powder.

In addition, Obama's administration opened the door much wider to private prison operators. From 2005 to 2011, the revenue from the federal government for the GEO Group, which by 2018 had become the world's largest private prison operator, skyrocketed from $138.8 million in 2005 to $640 million in 2011, an increment of 364%. The bulk of that revenue came from contracts to detain and monitor immigrants.[20]

The Trump Presidency

During the 2016 election campaign, Donald Trump announced, "I am the law-and-order candidate." His platform followed that law-and-order line. He supported the reinstatement of the death penalty, had little to say about modifying harsh sentencing laws, and was a great champion of the expansion of private prisons. In addition, he advocated a great reduction in immigrant visas and applications for amnesty while aggressively promoting the extension of the wall along the Mexican border. His narrative echoed the politics of fear of the early years of mass incarceration.

These policies were no surprise. Trump had a history. In his 2000 book, *The America We Deserve*, he claimed that "tough crime policies are the most important form of national defense." As president, he urged police to "not be too nice."

Yet while Trump pushed the law-and-order theme and "I love the cops" was a repeating slogan in his rallies, he also championed a very mild set of reforms encapsulated in the First Step Act of 2018. The First Step Act reduced mandatory minimums on some drug sentences, including the penalty for crack cocaine, lowered the three strikes penalty to 25 years instead of a life sentence, and banned the shackling of pregnant people in prison.

The First Step Act stirred lots of controversy. Criminal justice reform advocates, like the liberal think tank the Brennan Center in New York, argued that the act was "one step in the right direction for reducing mass incarceration in the United States." However, more radical groups like the National Council for Incarcerated and Formerly Incarcerated Women and Girls rejected the approach of the act. In a petition to Congress, Andrea James, the executive director of the council, offered a harsh critique of the act: "Making the conditions of imprisonment marginally better does nothing to address the crisis of mass incarceration. Instead of steps, we must think about leaps forward." For her, such leaps would include the repeal of the 1994 Crime Bill and the mandatory minimums and the "other policies that have led to mass incarceration of Black and Brown people and our children."

By 2021, more than 1,774,000 people were incarcerated in the United States.

"If I don't win, America's Suburbs will be OVERRUN with Low Income Projects, Anarchists, Agitators, Looters and, of course, 'Friendly Protesters'"[21]

DONALD TRUMP

2020

The War on Immigrants

The US claims to be a "melting pot"—a nation of immigrants is the national narrative. However, from the outset, the relationship of settler colonialists and other populations has been on a war footing.

While much of the population in the US today has ancestry from different parts of the world, the pathway for people here was not one based on voluntary movement through visas and passports and legal processes. Instead, millions of immigrants came to the US as a result of violence and forced labor.

A Key Component of the War on Immigrants Is the Issue of Labor

World War II was a key moment in establishing the connection between immigration and labor. The war enlisted much of the US labor force into the armed forces. In their absence, the hunt for workers to replace them went outside US borders, primarily to Mexico.

In 1942, the US government set up the Bracero Program, which opened the door to workers from Mexico to contract to work in US industry, primarily in agricul-

EUROPEAN SETTLEMENT OF AMERICA

The first immigrants' arrival was based on the forced removal and massacre of Indigenous Americans.

1619

1492

VIOLENT ENSLAVEMENT OF AFRICANS

From 1619 onward, the US enslaved and kidnapped Africans from the African continent.

ture. While thousands of workers did come from Mexico through the Bracero Program work permit process, many others found their way to US factories and fields without such clearance. Many employers were willing to turn a blind eye to a person's legal immigration status if they could obtain laborers who often worked at wages far below those of their US counterparts.

However, at times anti-immigrant sentiments, much like we have seen in the US in recent years, prompted the government to deport workers by force. For example, in 1953, the government initiated a deportation action called Operation Wetback, in which immigration authorities rounded up hundreds of thousands of people of Mexican origin, even some who were US citizens, and flew them back to Mexico.

Subsequently in the 1980s, under President Ronald Reagan, the federal government intensified the repression of immigrants by creating a system of detention centers, more appropriately called immigration prisons. Since that time, the war against immigrants has ebbed and flowed in its intensity, with the pendulum swinging toward deportation at certain moments, blocking the border at other moments, and then at others providing legal avenues for citizenship and

THE BRACERO PROGRAM

The US government set up the Bracero Program, which opened the door to workers from Mexico to contract to work in US industry, primarily in agriculture.

THE MEXICAN WAR

made millions of people into immigrants through the redrawing of boundaries via conquest.

1882   1953

1848   1942

THE CHINESE EXCLUSION ACT

Tens of thousands of Chinese laborers were forced to come the US to work on the railroads. To reduce the flow of immigrants from China, the US government passed the Chinese Exclusion Act.

OPERATION WETBACK

in which immigration authorities rounded up hundreds of thousands of people of Mexican origin, even some who were US citizens, and flew them back to Mexico.

work permits. This ebb and flow is largely related to the demand for labor from US employers.

A key moment in the War on Immigrants was the 1994 North American Free Trade Agreement (NAFTA). This treaty opened the door for US companies to buy farmland in Mexico, a practice the Mexican government had outlawed since the 1930s. US companies then bought up hundreds of thousands of acres of agricultural land in Mexico, often displacing local farmers and farm workers in the process. Many of these landless people saw going to the US as the only viable economic alternative. This massive flow of immigrants triggered anti-immigrant sentiment and legal repression by the administration of Bill Clinton.[22] Part of these changes included deporting people who had criminal convictions. The number deported due to their criminal record grew from 37,724 in 1996 to 90,426 in 2005. The total number of people deported during that time grew from just over 100,000 to more than a quarter of a million in 2005.[23]

After 9/11

The attacks on the World Trade Center on September 11, 2001, stoked the fires of anti-immigrant sentiment, particularly toward Muslims and people from the Middle East. The Patriot Act of 2001 led to the formation of Immigration and Customs Enforcement (ICE), a division under the newly formed Department of Homeland Security. The zeal for anti-immigrant measures resulted in the budget

NORTH AMERICAN FREE TRADE AGREEMENT (NAFTA)

The US buys up land in Mexico and displaces farmers and workers.

1980s

1994

CREATION OF DETENTION CENTERS

Under President Ronald Reagan, the federal government intensified the repression of immigrants by creating a system of detention centers, more appropriately called immigration prisons.

for ICE exceeding the combined budgets of the FBI, the CIA, the US Marshals Service, and the Drug Enforcement Administration.

Popular sentiment among the US population also inspired the expansion of a new project—the building of a wall along the US-Mexican border. Between 2006 and 2009, the US government spent $2.4 billion in the construction of 670 miles of border wall.[24]

The building of the wall went hand in hand with the expansion of the surveillance of immigrants. Under the Intensive Supervision Appearance Program (ISAP), thousands of immigrants came under electronic surveillance of various forms. Many were put on GPS ankle monitors, even though they had not been convicted of any crime. In addition to the use of electronic surveillance, ICE contracted with a number of companies like Thompson Reuters, LexisNexis, and Palantir to compile personal digital files on millions of immigrants. Some activists argue that these files are "weaponized"—used against the interests of immigrants.[25] Research by organizations like Just Futures Law and Mijente have revealed how the data on individuals can be shared with other law enforcement agencies or sold to private companies that use it to market goods or to highlight those deemed to be high-risk individuals.

In addition to this increased technology, we also saw a rapid growth in immigration prisons. Whereas in 1981 there were just 54 immigrants in such prisons, by 2011, the population had risen to over 32,000.[26]

US-MEXICAN BORDER WALL AND RISE OF ICE

The US government spent $2.4 billion in the construction of 670 miles of border wall. There was also a huge boom in ICE immigration prisons.

2001

2006

PATRIOT ACT

led to the formation of Immigration and Customs Enforcement (ICE), a division under the newly formed Department of Homeland Security.

PART 2

JOURNEY THROUGH INCARCERATION

FOR EVERY 1 BORN, THERE ADMISSIONS IN THE US IN

In 2019, the US had 10.3 million admissions into jail.[27]

PERSON WERE 3 TO JAIL 2019.

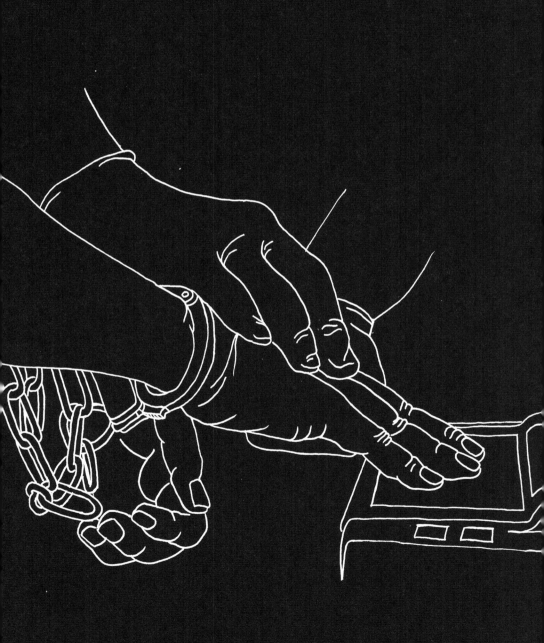

1. Jail and Sentencing

Jails are the local face of mass incarceration. Nearly every one of the more than 3,000 counties in the US has a jail. In many small counties, jails are the single biggest capital expenditure. These may range in size from the enormous Cook County Jail, which often houses more than 5,000 people, to lockups like the Dukes County (Massachusetts) Jail, which normally holds about 30 people.

While just under 2 million people may be behind bars at a given moment, in the course of a year some 11 million arrests will lead to incarceration. Like prison populations, the number of people held in jail during pretrial at a given moment has escalated during mass incarceration, from 182,745 in 2002 to 758,400 in 2019.[28]

During the pandemic, jail populations tended to fall, but many, especially in big cities, expanded again in 2021. Race plays a big part in how cases are handled at every step of the process. As in all aspects of mass incarceration, the jail population reflects racial bias. In 2020, Black people were jailed at the rate of 465 per 100,000 residents, as compared to 133 for whites.[29] A national study in 2018 concluded that Black people are 5 times more likely to be arrested than their white counterparts. But it doesn't stop there. In large urban areas, Black people are 25% more likely than white people to be held in jail during the pretrial period (the time between arrest and a court decision in the case). In addition, the bail amounts for Black people tend to be higher than those for whites.

For some people, short-term stays in jail may be a constant part of their life. These arrests may include traffic offenses, domestic violence, low-level drug use, and violation of "public decency" laws, such as urinating in a park or having an argument in a bar. For others, a trip to jail may just be the first stop in years or a lifetime of incarceration.

Next Spread:
Person carries mattress to cell in
St. Joseph County Jail, Indiana.
St. Joseph County Police Department

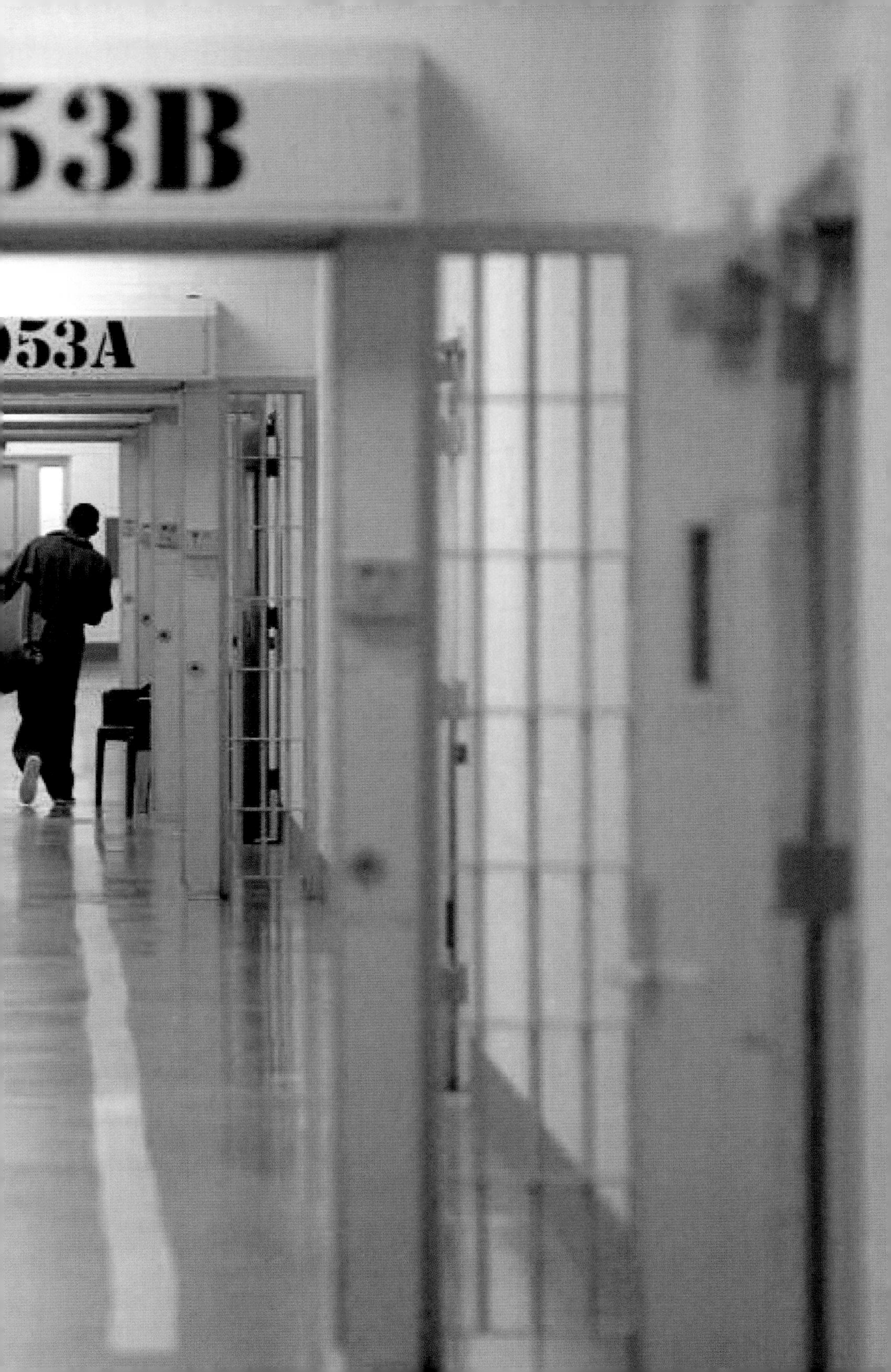
53B
53A

Arrest

Initial appearance
Accused is informed of charges
and assigned defense counsel.

Preliminary hearing
Judge determines if there is
probable cause to believe that the
accused committed the crime.

Bail hearing
Judge decides if the accused can
post bail and the amount of bail.
Black people are on average given
2x higher bail.

32%
**RELEASED ON
OWN RECOGNIZANCE**
Judge allows individual
to stay at home pretrial
without bail.

30%
PAID BAIL
Individual provides bail
amount and is allowed to
stay at home pretrial.

At home
pretrial

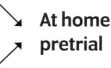

32%
CAN'T PAY BAIL
Individual cannot afford
bail and therefore has to
stay in jail.

In jail
pretrial
Approximately ¾ of
people in jail have
not been convicted
of a crime.

6%
DENIED BAIL
Court finds individual
dangerous or a flight risk
and denies the ability to
post bail.

From Arrest to Sentencing
Unfortunately, the most recent national pretrial
detention data is from 2004.

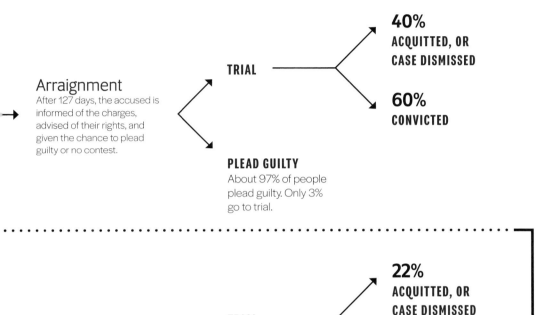

Arraignment

After 127 days, the accused is informed of the charges, advised of their rights, and given the chance to plead guilty or no contest.

TRIAL

40%
ACQUITTED, OR CASE DISMISSED

60%
CONVICTED

PLEAD GUILTY
About 97% of people plead guilty. Only 3% go to trial.

Arraignment

After 45 days, the accused is informed of the charges, advised of their rights, and given the chance to plead guilty or no contest.

TRIAL

22%
ACQUITTED, OR CASE DISMISSED

78%
CONVICTED
People detained pretrial are much more likely to be found guilty.

PLEAD GUILTY
People detained pretrial are even more likely to take the plea bargain.

The ability to afford bail greatly affects the chances someone is convicted.

Jails are packed with poor people.

Many people land in jail because of criminalization of their daily survival activities. This is referred to as the criminalization of poverty. Those who are unhoused are frequent targets of criminalization. In many jurisdictions, the law prohibits sleeping in public places. Several local authorities ban people from living in their car. Phoenix bans any camping in the city, even car camping. In Hawaii, a person cannot sleep or live in their car on any public roadway between 6 p.m. and 6 a.m. Cities like Las Vegas, Orlando, and Philadelphia have made it a criminal offense to feed people in public places.

Even people who avoid a jail sentence by being placed on an electronic monitor or going to drug court may end up back behind bars because they are unable to afford the user fees for these activities. In some jurisdictions, electronic monitors can cost a person up to $25 per day, plus a hookup fee of $200.

In many jurisdictions, criminalization of poverty enables aggressive, racially biased policing. Failure to pay fines or fees might land a person behind bars. Outdated car license registration or overdue traffic fines are often the result of the inability of the person to afford the charges. Data on traffic stops shows that Black and Latinx drivers are more commonly stopped by police than white drivers. In New York, a 2019 study found Black people were 6 times more likely to be the subject of "stop and frisk" by police and 6 times more likely to be arrested when they were stopped.

A survey of 980 Alabama residents who owed or were paying court debt showed 38% committed a crime to pay court debt.[30]

"Yeah, I got ticketed twice for sleeping under the Linden Street Bridge. I was sick, sleeping on a mattress under the bridge, and they woke me up and gave me a ticket. I balled it up and threw it in their face. 'F— you! I'm not gonna pay that. I can't pay that.' So I ended up in jail for failure to appear."[31]

JOEY FIALA

unhoused in Fort Collins, Colorado

Police evict and arrest homeless encampment in Minneapolis
A Powderhorn Park resident named Squad is arrested in front of his tent as a bulldozer stands by.
Ben Hovland for MPR News

Bail is not determined by ability to pay.

Bail imprisons the poor.

The original purpose of bail was to incentivize a person accused of a crime to attend their court appearances. In many countries, bail is a set of conditions that does not involve money at all. Instead of making payment a person may be compelled to meet with court officials, follow a curfew, present at a police station, or conform to travel restrictions rather than having to pay money. Under mass incarceration, cash bail has spread widely and the actual amounts of cash bail can be astronomical.

The realities of money bail mean that people are serving time in jail simply because they are poor and cannot afford the bail. In 2020, over 550,000 people were in jail who had not been convicted or sentenced. In 2020, the median bail for a felony was $10,000. Usually a person must pay 10% of that bail sum in cash. According to *Vox*, "In Philadelphia from 2008 to 2013, nearly 40% of those with bail set at $500 or less stayed in jail for at least three days."[32]

There is evidence that the amount of bail set by the judge is based entirely on the judge's discretion. Usually, the judge sets the bail within a few minutes. Judges set bail on average twice as high for Black defendants as for white defendants for the same severity of crime.[33]

In many places, courts follow **bail schedules**—amounts that are based on charge, without taking into account details of a person's case or their ability to pay, and often without defense counsel being present.

In 2022, Illinois became the first state to eliminate money bail. Under the state's Pretrial Fairness Act, a judge can either order a person to be freed pretrial or, if the judge deems the person a threat to themselves or to the community (or they are a threat to flee prosecution), they can be held in jail.

Bail Bond Industry

In many cases when a bail amount is set, the person incarcerated cannot afford to pay the entire amount. In such cases, they give 10% of the bail to a bail bond company, which puts up the remaining 90%. When the case is resolved, the bail bond company keeps the 10% as their profit. Bail bonds are big money, with more than 15,000 bail bond agents making a total profit of over $2 billion dollars a year. In recent years, many communities have set up community bail funds. A key goal of these funds is to end the incarceration of people because of poverty. These community bail funds raise money that they use to pay the bail for people to get them released. The bail fund then collects the money from their client once the case is over and then uses the same funds to bail out another person. There are over 90 community bail funds in the US. "They and their families are also targets for the $2 billion-per-year for-profit bond industry, which routinely exploits people—disproportionately people of color—in desperate situations."[34]

Bail is determined either by bail schedule or by a judge's discretion. Black and Brown defendants are given bail amounts twice as high as white people, even though they are less likely to be able to afford it.[35]

What happens if you can't afford bail?

STAY IN JAIL UNTIL ARRAIGNMENT
Increases chances of being convicted, as well as increases chances of false confessions.

TAKE A BAIL BOND
Pay a nonrefundable 10% of the bail to the bond agent and put up belongings as collateral.

97% of people take the deal

In the federal system, only about 3% of cases go to trial. Similar figures prevail in many parts of the country. The rest are resolved through plea agreements, what people in prison refer to as "taking a deal." In a plea agreement, a person consents to plead guilty to a charge and accept a sentence that is less than the maximum.

In most jurisdictions, if a person refuses a plea bargain and then loses a trial, they receive a much harsher sentence than what was offered in the plea bargain. To avoid a long sentence, many people accept a plea agreement even when they are not guilty or there is little evidence against them. Among Baltimore City drug cases in 2018, the average sentence for a person who pleaded not guilty but then lost their case in a trial was 7 times longer than for those who accepted a plea agreement.

You are arrested with 100 grams of crack. What do you do?

OPTION 1

GO TO TRIAL

You stay **6 months in jail and go to court.**

If found guilty, you will be given at least a **15-year sentence**, as that is the mandatory minimum.

You **can appeal** your case if found guilty.

People also accept plea bargains if they don't have enough money to hire a lawyer. Those who can't afford a paid lawyer receive a public defender. The quality of public defenders varies widely. Some are dedicated to their duties and do their best to represent their clients. Others are less interested or maybe have a very heavy workload that prevents them from spending an adequate amount of time on an individual's case.

Borjan Kovacevic, a Chicago defense attorney, stated that many of his clients plead guilty despite his advice because they are desperate to be free. "I knew for a fact they were innocent, but they're scared, they're getting beat up, and all they can think about is getting out of there," said Kovacevic.[36]

OPTION 2

TAKE A PLEA BARGAIN

You stay **6 weeks in jail.**

You agree to a **5-year sentence.**

You **cannot appeal** your case.

Jail has lasting impact.

Although the Constitution guarantees a "speedy trial," the reality is quite different. Some cases take months, even years to be resolved. In Alabama, between 2013 and 2017, felony cases on average took 168 days to be resolved; misdemeanors took an average of 81 days. For homicide cases, the statewide average was 364 days until resolution, but in Tuscaloosa County the average wait was 589 days.[37] During this entire time, the person remains in jail, without conviction. Many people plead out because of the strong negative impacts of jail.

Conditions in county jails are often far worse than in prisons. Most jails have few recreational facilities or programs, have very limited medical facilities, and offer few items in the commissary. In many jails, people are only let out of their cells a couple times a week to shower. Visiting facilities are typically through glass or via video technology, for which visitors must pay.

For those who cannot pay bail, remaining in jail has serious consequences. They may lose a job or be evicted from their residence. Moreover, many people in jail have parenting or other caregiving responsibilities that must be done by someone else while they are incarcerated, or alternatively children are simply left to suffer alone. If they require constant medical care, the jail is not likely to provide that.

Plus, remaining in jail during pretrial makes a person more likely to be convicted. A 2016 paper analyzing more than 420,000 cases determined that those who gained pretrial release were 15.6 percentage points less likely to be found guilty. Not surprisingly, prosecutors commonly condition plea offers on postponing hearings in which defendants may challenge their arrests and request release.

Kalief Browder was 17 when he was accused of stealing a backpack in a New York store.

He refused to accept the plea bargain, but his family could not afford his $3,000 bail. He remained in solitary confinement in Rikers Island jail for 17 months. He continued to refuse a plea bargain, insisting on his innocence.

Finally, he was released and the charges were dropped. However, the jail experience traumatized him severely. On June 6, 2015, he hanged himself.

His death sparked massive protests in New York and other cities. Kalief's mother died a little over a year later from a heart attack, but lawyer Paul Prestia, who had been involved in Kalief's case, said she died "of a broken heart."[38]

On May 25, 2017, the corner of East 181st Street and Prospect Avenue in the Bronx was renamed "Kalief Browder Way."[39]

Drawn by Robert A. Odom, incarcerated in North Carolina

AT LEAST
1/7

OF PEOPLE IN PRISON ARE SERVING LIFE SENTENCES.

Over 200,000 people are currently serving life sentences in state and federal prisons.[40]

2. Life in Prison

In the 1960s and 1970s, prisons had programs of rehabilitation—higher education courses were common, and job training also was often available. As criminologist Betsy Mathews put it in the 1980s, "Rehabilitation formed the basis of correctional practice." But mass incarceration involved shifting the underlying philosophy. Prisons increasingly were oriented toward punishment, the so-called punishment paradigm. A common term that justice advocates applied was "warehousing." Prisons became places where bodies were stored, waiting to be pulled off the shelf and sent back to the community. On the ground in prisons, this meant that guards, though they had advocated for changing their job title to "correctional officers," largely became disciplinarians rather than advocates and facilitators of rehabilitation. Their job became control and punishment. Rehabilitation had vanished from the ethos.

Next Spread:
California Institution for Men
In 2006, California Institution for Men was 97.5% over capacity.
California Department of Corrections and Rehabilitation, August 2006

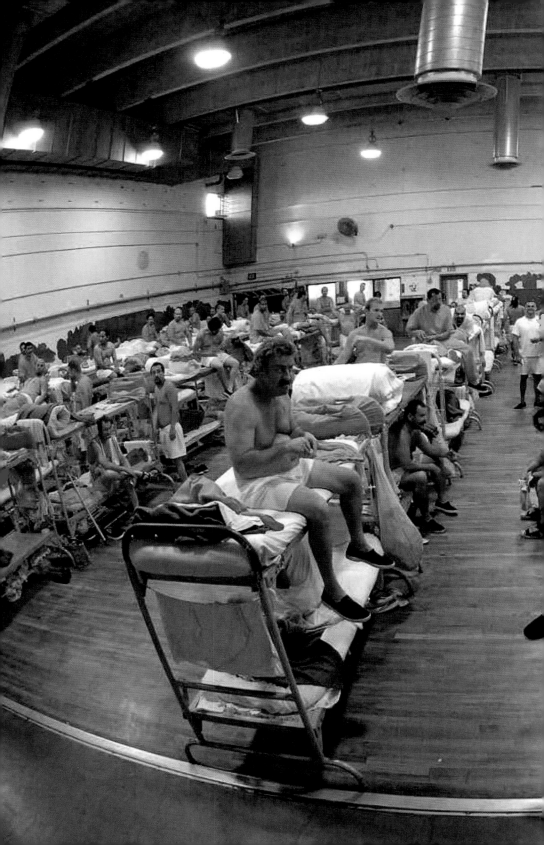

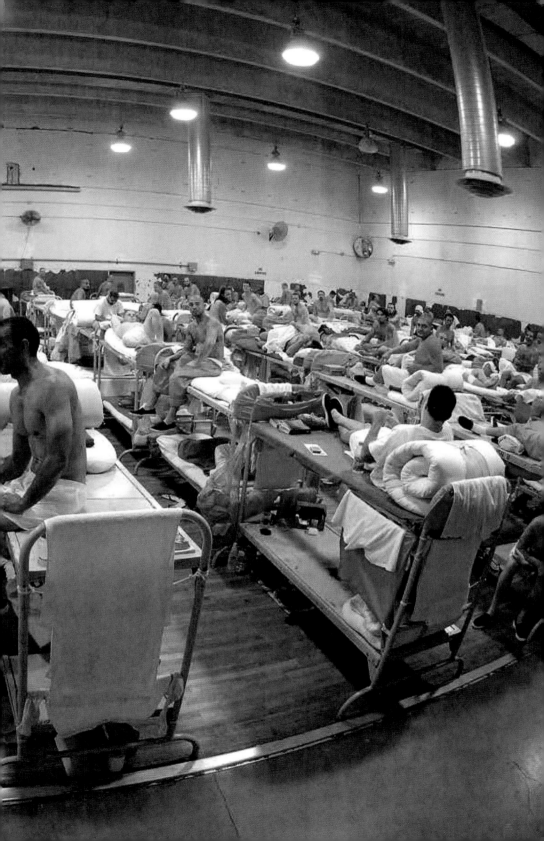

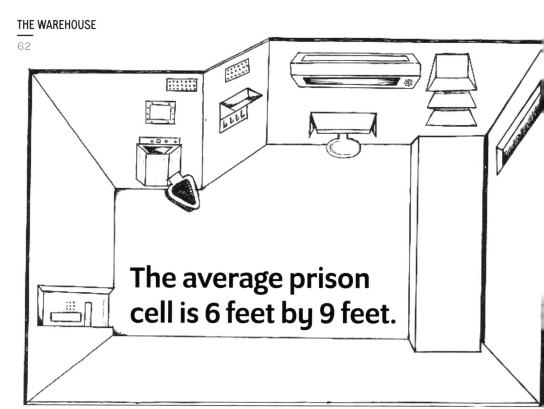

The average prison cell is 6 feet by 9 feet.

Prison and jails vary in terms of their physical layout. In the past, cells in many prisons were designed for one person. But in the era of mass incarceration, most cells accommodate two people. The most common structure is a box, as shown in the diagram, with a stainless steel toilet and sink and two bunk "beds," which are usually slabs of steel with a very thin mattress on top. Some cells are so small that a person standing in the middle can touch both sides at the same time. The doors vary. Older prisons have bars across the front, but more modern cells have a solid front wall with a heavy metal door that is opened remotely by a guard. Some have slots in the door through which guards can slide food trays or reach in to put a person in handcuffs before letting them out of the cell. But many prisons, especially lower security facilities, house people in dorms, which have multiple beds spread out across an open floor. As prisons became more crowded, authorities began using any available space as a "dorm." These included gyms, libraries, chapels, and warehouses. In some cases, people are put in tightly packed spaces and put in triple bunks.

Layout of a cell
Greg Curry, incarcerated in Ohio

Most prisons were built in the 1980s and 1990s. By now they are old, often deteriorating. Moreover, in the years since they were built the climate crisis has had an impact on the ecosystems where many of these prisons are located. For example, with the overall rise in temperatures, some people are "boiling behind bars," locked in cells without air conditioning where the temperature may reach 130 degrees. The proliferation of storms and rising waters threatens many prisons that lie near coastlines or other bodies of water. In 2021, repeated storms in Florida meant that water flooded the prison blocks at the Cross City Correctional Institution in Dixie County, Florida. It became so severe, they had to evacuate the prison. DaRon Jones, who was incarcerated there, described the situation: "The water was close to ankle deep, with human waste floating by as we were fed in our cells. The smell was unlike anything I have ever encountered." By the time they moved out of the prison, he reported that "the water was knee deep with snakes and bugs swimming in the water."[41]

A day in a minimum security prison[42]

6 a.m.	wake up
7 a.m.	breakfast and travel to work site
8 a.m.	work
11 a.m.	lunch
12 p.m.	work
3 p.m.	travel to prison
4 p.m.	off duty/time on prison yard
5 p.m.	dinner
6 p.m.	religious or specialized programming
8 p.m.	return to dorm and remain in housing area
11 p.m.	lights out

Life Sentences

More than ⅔ of those serving life sentences are people of color; 1 in 5 Black men in prison is serving a life sentence.

Today over 200,000 people are serving life sentences in US prisons, more than the entire incarcerated population in 1970. About 30% of those serving life sentences are older than 55. Many of these individuals have a life-without-parole sentence, a penalty that does not exist in any other country. Also, in 2016, more than 44,000 people were serving virtual life sentences—a sentence that they could not complete before death. Virtual life typically includes sentences of 50 years or more. It is often called "death by incarceration."

In recent years, advocates and incarcerated people have stepped up their efforts to overturn or modify life sentences to get people out of prison, especially those who have served long terms. The Illinois Prison Project has been active in fighting for commutations for people with long sentences. As of 2022, their work had secured the release of 70 people from Illinois prisons, including Renaldo Hudson, who was given a death sentence that was commuted to life in prison in 2009. He secured a commutation of his sentence in 2020, after serving 37 years in prison.

Hudson committed a murder at age 19 while he was high on drugs. He was initially sentenced to death, but that sentence was later reduced to life without parole. Hudson would end up spending 37 years in Illinois prisons, during which time he taught himself to read and then went on to complete a bachelor's degree. In 2020, Governor J.B. Pritzker granted him executive clemency. Hudson was released from prison, and he immediately began to do work with other people who had come home from prison.

Mumia Abu-Jamal, originally sentenced to death for a conviction for the murder of a police officer in 1981, successfully fought to get his Pennsylvania sentence reduced to life in prison without parole. But Mumia maintained his innocence and built an enormous following across the US and Europe in support of his efforts to be free. Saint-Denis, a suburb of Paris, France, named a street after Mumia in 2006. Over the years, Mumia wrote several books and was a frequent commentator on radio broadcasts, pushing back against his conviction and the use of life imprisonment.

"After 37 years in prison, I was not the broken teenager that was sentenced to die at the hands of the state.

My transformation may look dramatic, but it is no way unique. Just as I was, there are now thousands of people sitting in cells throughout Illinois who have spent years growing, learning, and changing. Just as I was, they are ready to return home. Without parole or mid-sentence review, there is no recognition within the criminal legal system that people change or grow. There has to be room for mercy and justice to sit together."[43]

RENALDO HUDSON

Illustrated by Kenneth Reams, incarcerated in Arkansas

Solitary Confinement

80,000 people are in solitary in the US.[44]

Most prisons and jails make use of some form of solitary confinement as a punishment or method of separating people from the general population. Solitary confinement usually means locking a person in a cell alone for 22 to 24 hours a day.

Common reasons given by authorities for isolating people are incidents of violence, protection from other people in the population who may want to harm them, or separating people who may have a contagious disease like HIV/AIDS. Transgender people are particular targets for solitary. In fact, Layleen Polanco Xtravaganza, a trans Afro-Latina, died in solitary in New York's Rikers Island jail in 2019. She passed away when she had a seizure.

However, evidence does not always support official explanations for use of solitary. In fact, a 2016 report by the Vera Institute found that 85% of the thousands of people held in solitary in Illinois prisons were placed there for "minor infractions such as abusive language."[45]

Historically, the US has been one of the few countries in the world to use solitary confinement in juvenile prisons, though this practice has been greatly reduced or eliminated in many states in recent years.

Authorities use many terms for solitary confinement: administrative segregation, special housing, secure housing, restrictive housing, behavior modification, or simply isolation.

As of 2021, a Yale study concluded that more than 40,000 people in US prisons and jails were in solitary confinement.[46] The United Nations has determined that keeping someone in isolation for more than 15 days is a form of "torture" and can have serious long-term mental health consequences. In 2021, the Yale report estimated about 6,000 people had been in solitary for over a year. Many prisons subject people to solitary for decades.[47]

Conditions in solitary confinement vary. In some units, the incarcerated person may not have access to books or TV. Access to phones as well as visiting may be restricted or disallowed. Many solitary units have exercise spaces, where a person may be able to exercise for an hour a day. These are often called kennel runs, because they resemble the cages in which dogs are often held.

"Most of you out there will never experience this hell called solitary confinement.

So you'll never understand the tormented mind. You will never comprehend the daily struggles that an individual goes through. Where at times you're struggling to get through not another day, not an hour, but just another minute. You can read about this until you're blue in the face. I can describe it in great detail, but you still would not grasp the daily psychological hell that we endure."[48]

RONALD CLARK

has been in solitary confinement on death row for 31 years in Florida. He spends 23 hours a day in a 9-foot-by-7-foot cell.

Photo Requests from Solitary

These photos are the result of a project started by Tamms Year Ten that connected image requests from people in solitary confinement to volunteers on the outside. To learn more and to help fulfill requests, go to photorequestsfromsolitary.org.

I love (frogs) because I used to catch them when I was young. I just want a Photograph of a nice frog a (frogs) surrounded by rocks & Grass

Requested by Samantha
Photo by Maxine Collins

AN (early) sunset over water, the kind with lots of red and purple in the sky / clouds — ideally with a lone bouay in the distance.

Requested by Garry
Photo by Jessica Posner

WE WILL MAKE A
PHOTOGRAPH FOR YOU

Name: CHRIS ▮▮▮ JR
Date: October 10th 2013. Thursday.

Would you like to request one?

If so, fill out this form and describe a photograph you personally would like to receive.
A volunteer will make a photograph based on your description below.

You may request a photograph of anything (that is not prohibited by prison rules, of course).
In the space below, please describe what you would like to see in your photograph. (You could
describe a person, place, object, scene or idea.)

I would love to see the #1 thing I've not been blessed to see as of yet BARCLAY center in downtown BROOKLYN. It's been built since my incarceration. It just shows the way life still goes on + grows while we are away.

Do you have any specific instructions for the photographer?

I just want to see it the best way the photographer can capture it. To way I feel as I'M Right There. # BROOKLYN we go hard.

Organizations working to end the use of solitary confinement may use your photograph or
request for purposes of public education, media use or fundraising. If so, we could use your
name or you could remain anonymous.

If you would like us to use your name, what name should we use?

CHRIS ▮▮▮ jR

Requested by Chris
Photo by Erin Shirref

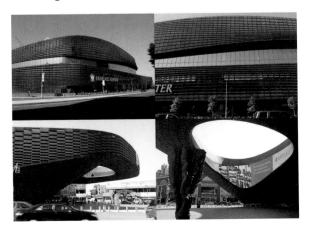

Sexual Assault in Prison

It's not what TV tells you.

One of the most dehumanizing stereotypes of prison life is the notion that men in prison are constantly raping each other. The phrase "Don't drop the soap," referring to dropping the soap in a shower in a men's prison, has become almost a cliché.

While sexual assault is part of the reality of prison, it has little to do with dropped bars of soap. According to research done by Interrogating Justice, "Most rape and sexual assault allegations point the finger at staff."

Despite the bar-of-soap intimations, the highest rate of sexual abuse comes from women's prison, with male staff being the primary offenders. The problem became so pervasive at the women's federal correctional institute in Dublin, California, that the population nicknamed the institution the "rape club." Allegations of sexual assault led to the firing of the warden at Dublin, Ray Garcia. He and three staff members were criminally charged for sexual assault. Garcia allegedly forced women in the prison to strip naked while he took photos of them. Pictures he had taken of the women were found on his phone during the investigation.

In the early 2000s, the Federal Bureau of Prisons identified sexual assault as a serious problem. Data gathered by authorities, along with grievances filed by people in prison, led to the passage of the Prison Rape Elimination Act of 2003 (PREA). This act mandated a zero-tolerance policy for sexual assault and compelled prisons to officially document every reported sexual assault. PREA did not absolutely ban consensual sex between incarcerated people, but it did give individual facilities the authority to ban all sexual activity in their institution. According to PREA, no sexual interaction between a staff member and an incarcerated person can be classified as consensual.

While PREA has had some impact, incidents of sexual abuse in prison are difficult to quantify. Many go unreported due to shame or fear of retribution. Until 2012, there were few regulations defining sexual assault in prisons. But a directive from the Justice Department in 2012 expanded the ways people in prison could report sexual assault and compelled authorities to investigate every allegation. As a result, reports of sexual assault rose from 8,768 in 2011 to 24,661 in 2015. About 58% of the reported incidents were accusations against staff. But while the number of reports grew astronomically, the percentage that was classified as "substantiated" shrank. Many people have expressed skepticism at this alleged number of false reports, as incarcerated people do not benefit and sometimes suffer greatly for coming forward.[49]

Whether carried out by a staff member or another incarcerated person, LGBTQ+ individuals are the most likely to be victimized. A California study found that transgender women in men's prisons were 13 times more likely to be sexually abused than the rest of the population. The act of housing a transgender person in a facility not designed for their gender identity could also be considered a form of sexual assault.

The most common sexual assaults are the strip searches by staff that every person endures every time they leave or reenter the prison. These searches have been the subject of lawsuits from incarcerated individuals, claiming that they violate the 4th Amendment. In Cook County, Illinois, 150,000 people who had passed through the jail were awarded up to $200 each for the violation of their 4th Amendment rights due to strip searches between 2002 and 2009.[50]

In 2020, people incarcerated at Lincoln women's prison in Illinois won a suit against the Illinois Department of Corrections for an incident in 2011 in which women were forced to stand naked for several hours while trainee guards practiced handcuffing and searching them.

"It is hard to fully explain how this felt.

The captain who already had complete control over my day-to-day life was now enforcing that control over my body and using my desire to see my child to threaten me to stay silent. ... I was sentenced and put in prison for the choices I made. I was not sentenced to being raped and abused while in prison."[51]

BRIANE MOORE

who testified in a Senate hearing on sexual abuse in federal prisons in 2022

The Mental Health Impact of Incarceration

According to a 2017 report from the Bureau of Justice Statistics, ½ of those in prison and ⅔ of those in jails had either "serious psychological distress" or a history of mental health challenges.[52]

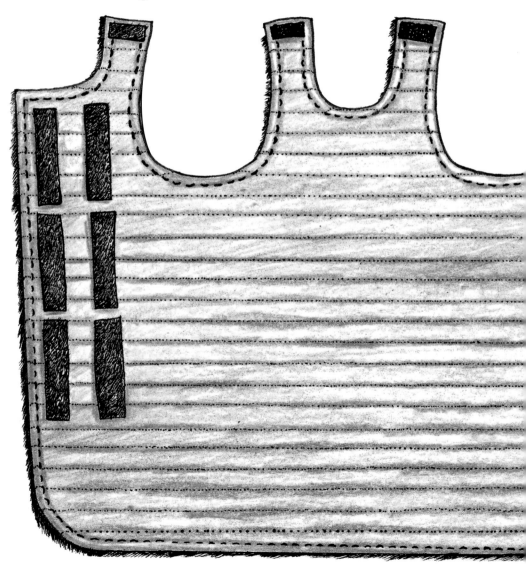

**Suicide prevention smock
(turtle suit)**
This smock is distributed to people on suicide
watch to wear instead of their own clothing.
It is tear-resistant in order to prevent
individuals from using their clothing to form
makeshift nooses.

Suicide is the leading cause of death in jails.[53]

All too often, mental health services in prison consist of providing a person with antidepressants or other psychotropic drugs, which primarily aim to keep the person pacified rather than to help them address any underlying issues. Plus, many incarcerated people view prison mental health providers as part of the system and may be hesitant to share any personal details with them for fear of being punished. Often if a person in prison engages in self-harm or threatens suicide, they will be put on suicide watch, which usually means being put naked in a cell alone, with just a blanket and maybe a thin mattress, with a guard stationed outside the cell doing the watching. Dr. Craig Haney testified in court that he found Alabama's "therapeutic cells" indistinguishable from the harshest solitary confinement cells.

"I refused to wear the smock, so I wore nothing but my birthday suit. I couldn't be humiliated more than I already was."[54]

JEFFREY MCKEE

a writer incarcerated in Washington

Prison, especially for those serving a long sentence, has deep mental health impacts on individuals. People in women's prisons and jails are more likely to have a history of mental health problems than those in men's facilities. Researchers are only beginning to explore this process, which many people now refer to as post-incarceration syndrome. The mental health impact may vary from individual to individual, often depending on what prison they are in and the dynamics of the population in that prison, as well as the mental health of the person when they entered the prison.

Out of the people who met the threshold for serious psychological distress, only 40% of state-incarcerated people and 26% of federally incarcerated people were able to access treatment in prison.[55]

Some mental health effects
of incarceration include:

The rise of antisocial traits

Prison is often a hostile environment, eliciting rage, resentment, and interpersonal violence. These are likely to emerge, particularly if the person experiences abuse or hostility from guards or other incarcerated individuals; these may be enhanced by racism and/or gender-based aggression derived from homophobia or transphobia.

Long-term feelings of helplessness

The power of the prison as an institution may lead a person to believe they are powerless to shape their destiny.

Sensory deprivation

If a person is in solitary confinement or a prison that has frequent lockdowns due to violence, they may not feel comfortable outside or in a space with lots of people.

Difficulty in expressing emotions

Incarcerated populations, especially in men's prisons, may view expressions of vulnerability such as crying or caring as weakness rather than an acceptable response to prison conditions. This promotes a reticence for people to talk about feelings or emotional pain.

Feelings of rage or despair

Many people, especially if they did not commit the crime with which they are charged or are facing very long sentences, may feel anger or despair because of their situation.

Institutionalization

Prison life consists of a repetitive routine that may make it difficult for a person to adjust to any changes in that routine.

COVID-19 in Prison

During the first year of the pandemic, the death rate for incarcerated people was more than 3 times that of the general population.

The COVID pandemic, which struck the world most fiercely in 2020–21, had a serious impact on incarcerated populations. From the outset it was clear that given the highly contagious nature of the virus, jails and prisons would become hot spots for the spread of the disease. The recommended methods to control the virus—social distancing, hand washing, wearing of masks, and, in the end, the implementation of regimes of testing and vaccinations—were all extremely difficult for people behind bars.

While many jails did release people to enable some social distancing, prisons were extremely slow to take action. Only 3 states—New Jersey, California, and North Carolina—released a significant number of incarcerated people from prisons. Parole boards also approved fewer releases in the first year of the pandemic than the year before. The response of governments was so ineffective that, in total, 10% fewer people were released from prisons and jails in 2020 than in 2019. Moreover, in another attempt to limit the spread of the pandemic, most prisons suspended visits during COVID-19, intensifying the isolation of incarcerated populations.

Even when provisions like hand sanitizer and masks were available, quite often they weren't shared among the population. In some cases, prison personnel expropriated personal protection equipment for themselves or family members. In many other instances, prison staff themselves refused to wear masks or seek vaccinations, making corrections employees one of the key sources for actually spreading the virus.

Data from the UCLA Law COVID Behind Bars Data Project, the Marshall Project/Associated Press, and other sources estimated that the percentage of prison staff who had received at least one COVID-19 vaccine dose was only 48%. In states like Michigan and Alabama, just over 10% of staff had gotten at least one dose of a COVID-19 vaccine by early 2021. All this contributed to the death of many people behind bars.[56]

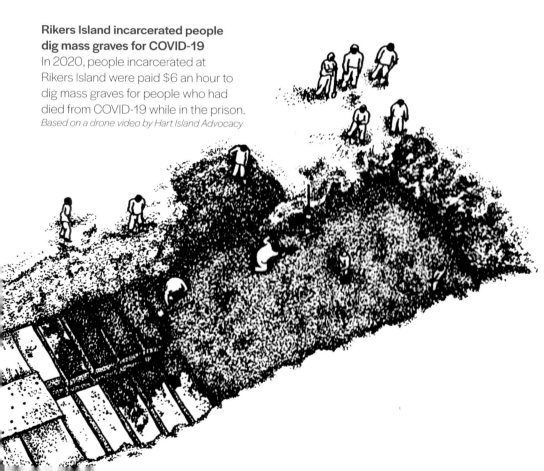

Rikers Island incarcerated people dig mass graves for COVID-19
In 2020, people incarcerated at Rikers Island were paid $6 an hour to dig mass graves for people who had died from COVID-19 while in the prison.
Based on a drone video by Hart Island Advocacy

"They posted signs down by the phones instructing us to put a sock—yes, like you wear on your foot—over the phone receiver before using it in order to avoid spreading germs."[59]

CHRISTOPHER BLACKWELL

incarcerated in Washington

COVID-19 thus added a new dimension to the punishment of the US criminal legal system. As the Vera Institute noted, "Most incarcerated people in the United States were left behind bars in dangerous conditions during the pandemic, even though public health experts recommended safely releasing people as the best way to prevent the spread of COVID-19."

Prisons were also slow to distribute anti-COVID medications like Paxlovid. The federal government allocated 160 doses of the drug to federal prisons authorized by the FDA in December but after 6 months had only distributed 3 doses.[57]

The Prison Policy Initiative states, "At the onset of the pandemic, areas with higher incarceration rates experienced significantly higher COVID case rates. Our analysis showed that in the summer of 2020, mass incarceration resulted in half a million more cases nationwide. The study revealed that not only do prisons not improve public safety, they also harm public health."[58]

"And that place is dangerous. It is a death sentence to detainees, especially right now with the coronavirus.

Medical attention is very poor, at best. The conditions there are filthy. The staff are very aware of the dangers and the dire situation that they have us all in, and they just don't care. They don't care about our safety. They don't care about our well-being. And it's clear in the way they treat us and in the hygiene kits and the food and the water that they provide us. It's a clear signal of their poor treatment and negligence towards us."[60]

JOE MEJIA

Joe Mejia was held for 11 months by ICE in Yuba County Jail. He led a hunger strike against the conditions of the ICE detention center, especially with regard to the dangerous COVID conditions the people were placed in.

Illustrated by Sean Fox, incarcerated in Texas

1 OUT OF 3

US ADULTS HAVE A CRIMINAL RECORD

The Sentencing Project

3. Release

From day one people face an uphill battle upon release.

A person's transition from prison largely depends on how much support they have from their family and community upon release. Having a family able to financially and emotionally support a person greatly enhances chances for success. But far too many families with incarcerated loved ones lack these resources. People who go to prison are generally poor. In 2017, 63% of people on probation came from a household with an income of less than $20,000. Many people coming home may have another family member who is incarcerated or caught up in fighting criminal charges. Since Black people are incarcerated at 5 times the rate of white people and twice the rate of those labeled "Hispanics," systemic racism is also something many people from prison must confront.

People who come out of prison are typically put on a system of supervision called parole. Typical terms of parole span 3 to 5 years but in some cases extend up to 30 years. Those coming out of jail usually are put on probation, a local form of supervision that usually lasts about a year or two.

Out the Door

Being released from prison or jail does not immediately free a person's mind from the impact of incarceration. Being locked up is a traumatic experience. People carry emotional and sometimes physical scars from prison, especially if they have been in prison for a lengthy period. They need healing and care to prosper.

Gate Money

Prisons do very little to prepare people for this transition. Most prisons provide "gate money"—a small cash payment upon release. In Illinois, gate money is $10. In California, it is $200. In North Dakota, the prison deducts money from the wages of a person's prison job and puts it into a "release aid account," which they receive upon release. If the person has not worked while in prison, they receive no gate money. Most prisons will provide a one-way bus ticket to a person's home jurisdiction if they have no one to pick them up at the gate. They may receive minimal clothes, like sweatpants, T-shirts, and slip-on canvas shoes.

Gate money
In Illinois, people get only $10 upon discharge to make it to their next destination.

Transition Housing

Halfway houses are part of the carceral system.

One of the few supports the prison system offers to people to prepare them for release are halfway houses. These are typically places where a person may live during the closing months of their sentence. The federal government contracts with about 150 of these nationwide. In most instances, a person is locked into the halfway house at night but may be free to work or visit people during the day. More common are transition houses—places where people who have completed their sentence live while they transition to the community. Most transition houses are privately owned. The operators of these facilities contract with local or state government for a fee.

Transition houses vary. Some, like Susan Burton's A New Way of Life in Los Angeles or Precious Blood in Chicago, offer comfortable housing and lots of support. Others are run by profiteers who contract for a short period of time, provide little or no support, and put people out on the street when the contract ends.

Probation and Parole

1 in 5 people in jail are there for a parole violation.[61]

Mass incarceration has not only imprisoned people but widened the net of those who are under surveillance and supervision by the criminal legal system. The two most important forms of surveillance by the criminal legal system are:

PAROLE

A program of supervision by the state directed at people who have completed a prison term. Parole is typically for a specific period of time, about 3 to 5 years, but some people are on parole for life.

PROBATION

A program of supervision by local authorities such as counties or parishes. People on probation usually either have finished a short sentence in a county jail or may be placed on probation instead of doing time in a jail.

People under supervision generally have to follow a strict set of rules. These vary from state to state but typically mean: no use of illegal substances, drug testing, and mandatory attendance at groups or programs like anger management or parenting. People under supervision often have to pay a fee for these courses and programs. A person may also be compelled to seek and maintain employment and avoid past associates. They must meet regularly with their parole or probation officer and inform them if they change residence or employment or travel out of town. In some cases, probation or parole may be accompanied by tracking via a GPS ankle monitor, a cellphone tracking app, and house arrest. A violation of the rules can result in a person being sent back to prison or jail.

Historically, some parole and probation officers provided support and assistance to their clients, but in the era of mass incarceration their role has changed. Now, parole and probation officers largely focus on monitoring whether their clients commit any new crimes or violate the rules of their supervision. Instead of carrying portfolios of helpful information for their clients, many of them carry guns. They police far more than they support.

How to Violate Your Parole

1. Association

A person on parole often cannot associate with another person on parole or even a person with a felony. In many neighborhoods, this is a very difficult challenge.

2. Alcohol or Drug Consumption

Most people on parole have to take frequent drug tests. Many are not allowed to consume alcohol or even possess alcohol in their house.

3. Travel

Often a person on parole will be restricted to a county or not be allowed to travel more than 50 miles from their house without permission. Out-of-state travel is often forbidden.

4. Failure of a Search

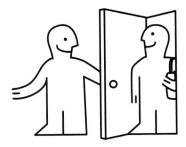

A person's place of residence, employment, and their person are subject to search 24 hours a day without advance notice. This includes what other members of the household bring into the home.

Electronic Monitoring and E-Carceration

Ankle monitors, or ankle shackles as some call them, come with many other problems, including:

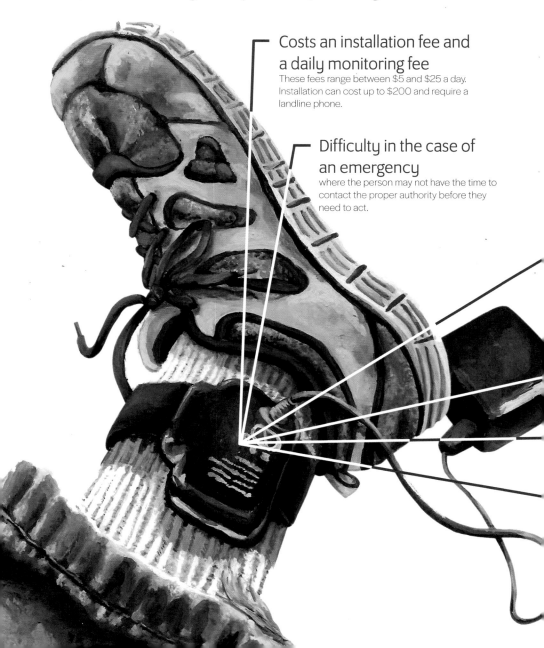

Costs an installation fee and a daily monitoring fee
These fees range between $5 and $25 a day. Installation can cost up to $200 and require a landline phone.

Difficulty in the case of an emergency
where the person may not have the time to contact the proper authority before they need to act.

Electronic ankle monitors first came into use in the 1980s. Judges and prosecutors viewed them as a soft alternative to prison. As their use spread, they seeped into every corner of the criminal legal system, used in pretrial release, postprison supervision, juvenile justice, and immigration and DUI cases. The first electronic monitors (EMs) simply told authorities whether a person was at home. But in the early 2000s, manufacturers added GPS tracking capacity to these devices. This meant the monitor could track you everywhere you went 24/7.

As the use of these devices has spread, the lived experience of being on a monitoring regime has led to an increasing critique of their use. In most cases, electronic monitors come with a strict regime of house arrest, requiring a person to get permission from a judge or a parole officer to leave their house for any purpose. Leaving the house without permission or returning later than the agreed-upon hour can lead a person back behind bars.

The assigned arrest site might be dangerous for the person
such as a place where they might be tempted to use substances or are subject to violence.

Needs to be charged every day for 2 hours
Failure to do so may result in inaccurate reporting and a reported violation.

Extremely inaccurate
These devices often incorrectly report that the person has left their house.

Strict hours for coming and going
make it difficult to take a job that might require unplanned overtime or changes in the work schedule.

Changing Technologies

While ankle monitors have been the standard piece of equipment for electronic monitoring, the present trend is to switch to cell-phone apps that track an individual. These apps not only track a person's location but also can open a person's entire phone contents to the authorities. Data captured via a cell phone can be shared with law enforcement or sold to vendors who want to promote their products to new customers. By 2022, more than 250,000 people under the authority of Immigration and Customs Enforcement were being monitored via a cell-phone app called SmartLINK, produced by BI, the largest electronic monitoring company in the US. BI is a subsidiary of the GEO Group.

Tyshontae Williams, who was on a monitor in New Haven, Connecticut, lamented, "I couldn't even take out the garbage; my mother actually made a point about that." Then he managed to get his rules changed slightly: "I got that little bit of freedom from my back porch to my trash can. It was annoying. ... My home was like a prison."[62]

E-Carceration

Electronic monitors are part of a set of technologies we call e-carceration. These technologies gather data in order to punish and control. Other technologies of e-carceration include facial recognition, license plate readers, street cameras, and shot spotters. This technology particularly targets working-class communities of color—Black, Brown, Indigenous—gathering data in order to build up files and information that help to criminalize their actions and their networks.

"If EM had given me more movement, I probably would have fought the case ... [but] my kids were not getting the healing that they needed. ... You're not even able to provide or do anything in your community let alone your family. It's not a solution."[63]

LAVETTE MAYES

who spent 121 days on an electronic monitor waiting for a trial in Chicago

"Almost no aspect of a person's life is unaffected. You are wearing a jail anywhere you go, on your leg, in your phone. It is a daily reminder that there are people who view you as sub-human."[64]

EMMETT SANDERS

on wearing an ankle monitor
after serving 22 years in prison

Adjusting to Life on the Outside

Incarceration is traumatic, but postprison life can also be traumatic. A set of legal and psychological barriers during transition can pose major challenges. Some people refer to this as post-incarceration syndrome, a condition much like the PTSD soldiers experience when returning to civilian life. While some social service agencies attempt to provide support to people coming home from prison, often the people working there have no experience of incarceration, no way of connecting to the traumas of their clients. Moreover, real barriers exist, especially for those with felony convictions and a long history of imprisonment. According to the Brennan Center, nationwide there are more than 45,000 state and local laws that limit the freedom of a person with a felony conviction. These "collateral consequences" include restrictions on employment, housing, access to public assistance, and parental rights.

Adjusting to the widespread use of technology, especially cell phones, is often challenging. But legal and policy restrictions that impact employment, housing, parenting, and access to food or medical care add to the difficulties.[65]

Finding Employment

Many employers don't hire people with felony convictions, especially a conviction that involves violence or is sexually related. Even if an employer is willing to hire a person who has been in prison, quite often they won't have a resume or skill set that makes them employable. Most prisons have cut back on training and education during the era of mass incarceration.

Incarceration Increases Unemployment[66]
Ages 35–44

4.3%

18.4%

WHITE MEN
become 4.2 times more
likely to be unemployed
after being incarcerated.

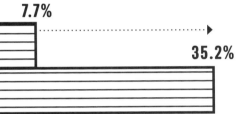

7.7%

35.2%

BLACK MEN
become 4.5 times more
likely to be unemployed
after being incarcerated.

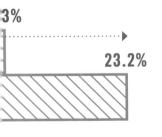

3%

23.2%

WHITE WOMEN
become 5.4 times more
likely to be unemployed
after being incarcerated.

6.4%

43.6%

BLACK WOMEN
become 6.8 times more
likely to be unemployed
after being incarcerated.

Voting Rights

Many states restrict or even eliminate the right to vote for people with felony convictions. In 19 states, people who are incarcerated lose their voting rights but can vote once they are released from prison. In 18 states, they must wait until they are off parole before they can vote. In 11 states, some people may lose their voting rights for life or may only get them restored by petitioning the governor. Just 2 states, Vermont and Maine (along with the District of Columbia), allow people in prison to vote.

Access to Aid

In many states, a felony conviction disqualifies people from receiving public assistance such as the Temporary Aid for Needy Families (TANF) or the Supplemental Nutrition Assistance Program (often called SNAP or food stamps). A study by the National Institutes of Health found that 91% of people released from prison said they experienced food insecurity. Public assistance, when available, can make a difference. Harvard Law School research found that access to TANF and SNAP reduced a person's chances of being reincarcerated by up to 10%.

"Without the ID nobody can do nothing for me. This is the longest I've ever been without a job. It's like they want you to go back to prison."[67]

MICHAEL ALBUJA

who was in an Illinois prison for 18 months

Acquiring ID

Most people leave prison with no driver's license or state ID. Without these documents, a person cannot access public assistance, housing, or employment. Just acquiring an ID may take several weeks or even months while a person scrambles to obtain copies of birth certificates or social security cards that they need to prove their identity. Some prisons have begun to provide people with ID documents upon release, but in most cases, the only ID they have is a prison ID, which is not widely recognized.

WHAT IS REQUIRED FOR AN ID UPON RELEASE:

1. MONEY

The mean cost of a state ID is $17.50, but it can cost even more if you need to take a driver's test beforehand.[68]

2. DOCUMENTS

Especially when someone has been incarcerated for a long time, it can be nearly impossible to find the necessary documents for a new ID like a birth certificate or social security card. Needing to replace one of these can take months of no employment.

3. TIME

The process of getting the ID from organizations like the DMV is often slow and opaque. "Trying to communicate with the DMV is like trying to talk to Martians on the moon. It's just impossible," said Zakee Hutchison, who was recently released in Los Angeles.

Finding Housing

Housing is another huge challenge for people coming out of prison. According to a report by the Prison Policy Initiative, **formerly incarcerated people are almost 10 times more likely to be unhoused than the general population**.

Many local jurisdictions allow landlords to discriminate against people with felony convictions who are seeking rental housing. Federal regulations ban people with certain drug offenses or sex-related offenses from living in public housing. Local laws may bar a person from living in a household with another family member who has a felony conviction.

In some states, the Department of Corrections doesn't release a person unless they have a residence that has been approved by a parole official. If a person can't find an approved residence, they can end up spending their parole time in prison, even though they have completed their sentence.

Rodney Gross spent 3 years in prison in Illinois after he had completed over 40 years behind bars because he could not find a place to live. It costs about $28,000 a year to keep someone in prison in Illinois, which means the Department of Corrections would rather spend $84,000 keeping him locked up than provide him with money for housing and let him out of prison. A 2015 study by the *Chicago Tribune* showed that over 1,200 people who had finished their sentence were being held in Illinois state prisons because they had no residence that the Department of Corrections would approve for their release.

The obstacles for people coming out of prison in finding housing are considerable. Many landlords use rating systems for applicants, which rate people on their income and recent rental record, automatically excluding people who have been in prison. Even federal programs that target unhoused people don't include people who have just been released from prison, because according to federal guidelines, a person who is in prison does not fit the criteria for being "unhoused." In their world, a prison cell is considered a house.

"Everyone I called ... they wanted to have a background check, the background checks [showed] the fact that I was a felon and they never called me back for approval of the application to rent from them. And I just got so frustrated I actually stopped trying."[69]

NASIR BLACKWELL

who tried to find housing in Chicago
after spending 24 years in prison

"A New Way of Life is a safe house that women can come to after they're released from prison in South Los Angeles.

It's a place for women to detox the trauma, the torture of incarceration, be welcomed and embraced and live and begin their new path to—if it's recovery or receiving mental health services, go back to school, get their children back."[70]

SUSAN BURTON

formerly incarcerated founder of A New Way of Life, a network of community houses for women returning home from prison
Drawn by Sean J. White, currently incarcerated

Returning to Family

Perhaps the most traumatic difference for a person coming out of prison is the changes their children have undergone, especially if the children had not visited their incarcerated parent frequently in prison. A person entering prison may have left behind a toddler or second grader who has now become a teenager or full-grown adult. The person coming home must deal not only with the shock of being back on the streets but with building a relationship with children they have never really known.

Plus, family members may have died during a person's incarceration, and the person in prison was unable to pay their respects. This leaves a void in a person that cannot easily be filled.

Family members may also be wary of a person who returns from prison. Maybe they remember things their loved one used to do before incarceration that caused harm. They may have no idea if the person experienced physical or sexual assaults while locked up or if they were involved in criminal or sexual activity in prison or what impact those experiences might have had on that individual.

Parenting and Child Custody

A period of incarceration gravely impacts a person's relationship with their children. Visits to prisons located in remote rural areas may be difficult or expensive. Charges for prison phone calls, which can be up to a dollar a minute, also restrict family connections.

In cases where people were not able to find family members to care for their children while they were incarcerated, their children usually end up in foster care. **Federal law states that if a child is placed in foster care for 15 months out of a consecutive period of 22 months, child welfare authorities can begin termination of parental rights.** In most cases, this leads to adoption.

According to a Marshall Project study, between 2006 and 2016 at least 32,000 incarcerated parents lost their children even though they had no history of physical or sexual abuse. **Incarcerated parents who had their children placed in foster care were more likely to lose custody of their children than those who physically or sexually assaulted their children, even though the former had no history of child abuse, neglect, or endangerment.**

Dorothy Roberts, author of *Torn Apart*, a study of racial disparities in foster care, argues that Black mothers are particular targets for losing custody of their children due to incarceration. Black children are 9 times more likely to have a parent incarcerated than white children, thus making them vulnerable to being placed in the foster care system or being put up for adoption.

Visitation
Stanley Jamel Bellamy's sons have grown up visiting him. He is sentenced to 65-plus years in a New York State prison.
Growing Up through Pictures

1 OUT OF 6

TRANS PEOPLE HAVE BEEN INCARCERATED

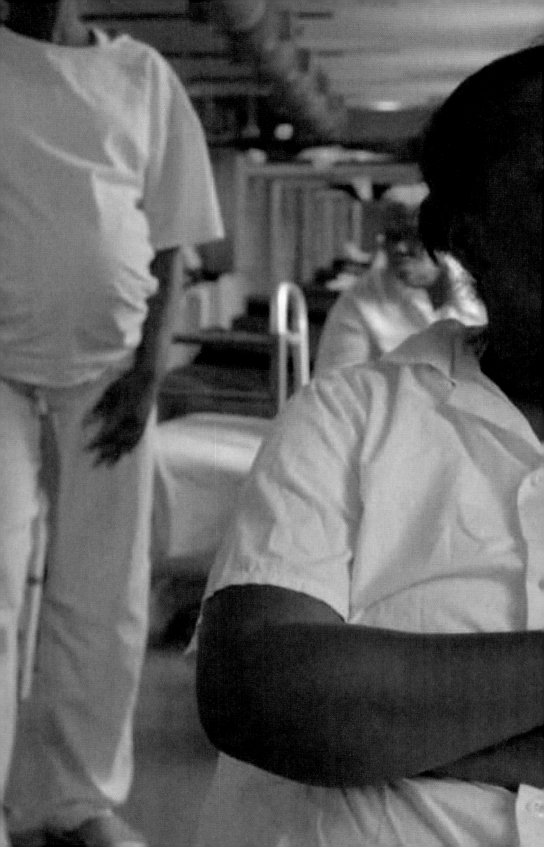

Marginalized in Prison

The overwhelming majority of the prison population is poor, with Black, Indigenous, and Latinx folks disproportionately targeted. Other marginalized groups are also overrepresented in the prison population and face their own particular challenges behind bars. Women often are denied adequate access to reproductive health, as exemplified by the struggle to access tampons or menstrual pads. Trans people are not only denied gender-affirming care and support but also face abuse and discrimination such as solitary confinement.

Though the Americans with Disabilities Act is supposed to guarantee equal treatment and accommodations, people with disabilities in prison face isolation, harassment, and especially poor medical treatment. Furthermore, as the population of people with long sentences meted out by mandatory minimums ages, more and more people are growing old in prisons without the equipment, support, or care they need.

Carrying a child in prison
The documentary *Tutwiler* examines the heartache and uncertainty faced by expectant mothers at a notorious women's prison in Alabama and the commitment of volunteer doulas to prepare them for delivery.
From Tutwiler, *by Elaine McMillion Sheldon, Alysia Santo, the Marshall Project, and PBS's* Frontline

Elders in Prison

Getting Old behind Bars

On average, more than 10% of people in state prison are 55 and older. This population grew by more than 400% from 1993 to 2013. By 2016, for the first time, those over 55 made up a larger share of the state prison population than those between 18 and 24. The growing number of elderly people in prison is largely a product of harsh sentencing legislation like mandatory minimums, enhancements, and truth in sentencing. The frequent imposition of life sentences played an important role as well. By 2019, more than 200,000 people were serving life sentences in state and federal prisons.[71]

Keeping elders in prison creates many problems. For instance, elders have more health issues than younger people. This increases the costs to the state of keeping such individuals behind bars and impacts their lives if they are eventually released. The absence of effective health care in prison ultimately means that incarcerated people tend to age faster than the rest of the population. One study in Pennsylvania showed that the health of a group of men in prison who averaged 57 years of age had a health profile comparable to men in the community who were 72.

"A friend of mine once pushed me in my wheelchair while returning from our meal. He is 91 years old and calls me a kid; I recently turned 56. When I asked him when he would be released, he ignored my question. I don't plan on asking again."[72]

ERIC FINLEY
incarcerated in Florida

In 2023, 1 in 5 incarcerated people are over 50 years old.[73]

Some prisons have addressed the issue of the elderly by creating separate yards for people over 55. In California Men's Colony in San Luis Obispo, authorities established the Gold Coat program, which trains incarcerated men to be caregivers for men on the yard who require care.

Release Aging People in Prison (RAPP), formed in 2013, campaigns to free long-serving elders from prison. RAPP views this as a method of fighting mass incarceration and promoting racial justice. They present themselves as being the only organization that focuses on "releasing aging people from prison rather than expanding additional resources to retrofit prisons as nursing homes." RAPP's mission states, "By organizing community power to free incarcerated elders, we work to uproot a system of endless punishment that fuels mass incarceration and damages Black and other communities of color."

"Our campaign focused on the elderly because they present the lowest risk of recidivism and if parole boards were really concerned about public safety, these are the people who should be released."

MUJAHID FARID

Mujahid Farid spent over 3 decades in prison. He paroled in 2011 and founded Release Aging People in Prison (RAPP), which helped gain freedom for elderly people. He led the organization until his transitioning in 2018.

Women's Prisons

The US imprisons a third of all imprisoned women in the world.

Between 1980 and 2019, the population in women's prisons increased by 700%. From 2008 to 2018 alone, women's jail populations grew 15%, while the figures for men's institutions declined by 9%. Although institutions labeled as women's facilities continue to grow, they still hold just slightly over 10% of the total incarcerated population. Moreover, people in women's institutions are about twice as likely as men to be locked up for a drug or property crime, as opposed to an offense involving physical violence. No simple explanation can account for this increase.[74]

1974   1976   1978   1980   1982   1984   1986   1988   1990   1992   1994

65

60

55

50

45

Who is incarcerated in women's prisons?

40

In addition, people incarcerated in women's prisons tend to have less serious charges than men. This means a much larger percentage of women are held in jails while awaiting trial as compared to men, the majority of whom are in state prisons. Even relatively minor charges that lead to a short jail stay can have a major impact on people in women's jails, who are more likely than men to have childcare and other family responsibilities.

35

People often enter a women's jail in an even more precarious situation than their male counterparts. They typically have lower incomes and are therefore less likely to be released on bail. Black women especially are targets for incarceration. At the turn of the century, statistics showed Black women were incarcerated at 6 times the rate of white women. By 2020, this ratio had fallen to 1.7 to 1.

30

25

Moreover, about a third of women admitted to jail have some form of serious mental illness, more than twice the rate of men. Much of this may be related to physical and sexual abuse, which an Illinois report showed was part of the life experience of at least 75% of women who entered prison. Incarceration is likely to exacerbate the trauma underlying that mental illness.

20

Crucially, around 80% of those held in women's prisons are mothers, and most are primary caretakers of children. Their mental state can have ripple effects on children and other people for whom women have caregiving responsibilities.[75]

15

10

1998   2000   2002   2004   2006   2008   2010   2012   2014   2016   2018

There are particular ways in which mass incarceration impacts individuals held in women's institutions. One report noted that ⅔ of reported sexual assaults by prison staff on the incarcerated come from women's prisons. The report noted that people in women's jails are more likely to leave having experienced additional harm, placing them back into the community in a situation in which they are more likely to end up back behind bars.

Several researchers have noted that prison and jail staff issue far more disciplinary "shots" against women than they do against men. These disciplinary actions often lead to the imposition of punishments like elimination of visits or phone calls, which are important lifelines for mothers and caregivers to children. A California study concluded that women got twice as many disciplinary write-ups as men for "disrespect."[77]

Provisions given to prison populations are often male-biased. For example, many prison or jail commissaries do not sell sanitary pads, grooming products, or any types of cosmetics. Medical services often overlook reproductive health needs or the special needs of people who may be pregnant.

Menstruation in Prison

Menstrual supplies in prison are frequently inaccessible, of poor quality, and withheld as a form of oppression and degradation. Because of the lack of supply as well as the poor quality of the pads, people often reuse pads past the point of medical safety or efficacy.

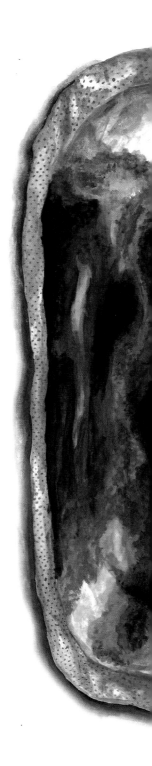

In one jail in Michigan, people were regularly denied access to the products and were forced to rewear bloodied clothing for up to a full week. In one case, prison staff ordered 30 people to share a pack of 12 pads.[78]

The menstrual products for sale in prison commissaries are unaffordable for most incarcerated people. For example, while incarcerated people in Florida earn on average less than 50 cents every hour, tampons cost $4 for 4 tampons. In Colorado, a box of tampons can cost about 2 weeks of wages. [79]

Most facilities require incarcerated people to ask the correctional officers for menstrual supplies, resulting in an immense power imbalance. In Rikers Island jail, a prisoner reported that a guard once "threw a bag of tampons into the air and watched as inmates dived to the ground to retrieve them, because they did not know when they would next be able to get tampons."[80]

The US Department of Justice investigation into the Julia Tutwiler Prison for Women reported that **correctional staff regularly withheld menstrual supplies in order to coerce prisoners into sex.** The report stated that "prisoners are compelled to submit to unlawful sexual advances to either obtain necessities, such as feminine hygiene products and laundry service, or to avoid punishment."[81]

Giving Birth in Prison

Taisie Baldwin gave birth to her daughter, Elaine, while she was in prison. According to prison policy, a mother could only keep her baby for 24 hours before it would be taken away.

"My perfect baby was born on June 25, 1998, after seventy-two hours of labor ... then they took me to a room on another floor. The guards were sitting next to my bed but they hadn't cuffed me yet. And then the nurse brought my baby back. ... The nurse had taken a few snapshots ... and she gave them to me. I was so happy I had the pictures. I knew I couldn't take my baby with me so it was the best I could have. ...

"The nurse took the baby while I went to get searched; after that she gave her back to me. By then I was sobbing and begging the guards, 'Please give me another minute.' But they kept saying, 'We have to leave, Baldwin.' I took a breath and gave the baby back to the nurse. ... For all I'd been through, leaving my baby at the hospital was the most painful thing I'd felt in my life. ...

"When I got in the van, one of the guards had to sit in the back with me. She told me, 'If you wanted to have children, you would have stayed out of prison.' I wanted to hurt her so badly but there was nothing I could do."

From *Inside This Place, Not of It*[76]

"We don't stop being a mother just because we are incarcerated but our families are not educated or made aware of the importance of keeping a mother close to the family. ... You've got to keep that relationship going."

DEBRA BENNET-AUSTIN

incarcerated in Florida for 19 years

Sharing baby pictures
The documentary *Tutwiler* explores the journey of giving birth in Alabama's Tutwiler Prison. Incarcerated mothers share pictures of their babies who were born in prison. They are only allowed 24 hours with the babies after giving birth.
Image from Tutwiler *by Elaine McMillion Sheldon, Alysia Santo, the Marshall Project, and PBS's* Frontline.

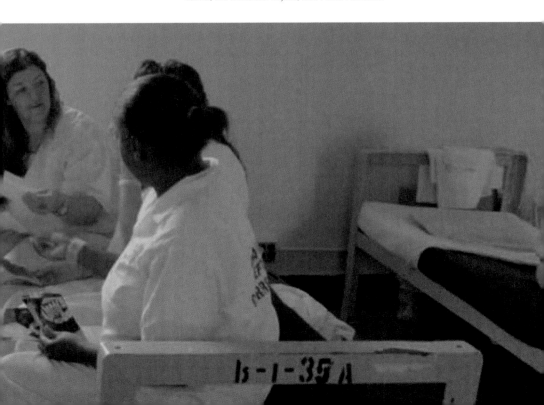

Being LGBTQ+ in Prison

People who self-identify as lesbian, gay, bisexual, transgender, or other gen-der-nonconforming identities (+) are often ignored in analyses of prison popula-tions. Unbelievably, the most recent survey of this population took place in 2012. The survey concluded that 1 in 3 people in women's prisons identify as LGBTQ+. In men's prisons, 1 in 20 people identify as LGBTQ+. Nearly half of all Black trans people have experienced incarceration.

Several factors contribute to the criminalization of LGBTQ+ people, including: police bias, anti-trans laws, anti-LGBTQ attitudes, the failure of schools to offer safe space for LGBTQ+ students, and discrimination in setting bail. Some activists label these practices as a "discrimination-to-incarceration pipeline" that channels LGBTQ+ people into disproportionate levels of imprisonment, particularly among youth. Twenty percent of those in the juvenile legal system are LGBTQ+.

Many facilities respond to harassment and assault of LGBTQ+ people by placing those who have been harmed in solitary confinement, allegedly for their protection, but usually to the great detriment of their mental health.

Transgender people often require special hormone therapy or gender-affirming surgery. However, to receive these therapies requires an examination, which is usually denied. A survey by Black and Pink, an abolitionist organization that provides service and support to incarcerated LGBTQ+ folks, found that only 1 in 5 incarcerated LGBTQ+ people had access to underwear and cosmetics that matched their gender identity.

In 2013, CeCe McDonald, a Black transgender woman, killed a man who was harassing and threatening her and her friends outside a bar in Minneapolis. Originally charged with manslaughter, authorities reduced the charges to second-degree manslaughter. McDonald plead guilty and served 19 months in a men's prison. Upon her release, she became a high-profile activist campaigning for the rights of transgender people and for reforms of the criminal legal system, including the right of an incarcerated person to define their gender.

"They wanted to force me to be someone that I wasn't. They wanted me to delegitimize myself as a trans woman and I was not taking that.

As a proud black trans woman, I was not going to allow the system to delegitimize, hyper-sexualize and take my identity away from me."[82]

CECE MCDONALD

formerly incarcerated
trans activist

Life as a trans person in prison is difficult and often traumatic.

The high incarceration rate of transgender people is directly related to the criminalization of survival activities. According to the Black and Pink survey, 1 in 5 transgender people had participated in the underground economy, including sex work and drug sales. Nine out of 10 of those who did sex work reported high levels of police harassment, sexual assault, or mistreatment by the police. Encounters with the police frequently led to conflict over gender identity, a conflict that persisted inside the prison.

About 1 in 10 trans people experience sexual assault from staff.

Almost a quarter of those reported sexual assault occurring 8 times or more. Nearly 1 in 5 trans people who were incarcerated had experienced physical assault from staff 8 or more times in the past year.

Other individuals among the incarcerated population also carried out verbal and sexual assaults against transgender people. Trans folks were 9 to 10 times more likely to experience sexual assault from other incarcerated individuals than the general population in the facility.

Transgender people in immigration detention facilities experienced similar rates of assault by staff and other incarcerated individuals, with 23% having survived sexual or physical assault while being locked up.

About 1 in 20 people in prison identify as trans.

**Daisy Meadows was given
60 days of solitary for
stuffing her bra with socks**
Daisy Meadows is a 27-year-old
trans woman incarcerated at
Lovelock Correctional Center. [84]

Only 15 out of 4,890 transgender people in prison
were assigned their lived gender rather than the
gender assigned at birth.[83]

Trans people or individuals who identify as nonbinary are often placed in an
institution that corresponds to their assigned gender at birth rather than their
chosen gender identity.

Roughly ⅓ of those incarcerated in prisons of any type
were denied access to prescribed hormone therapy.

85% of transgender people in all prisons have been
placed in solitary confinement.

Of those, nearly half had spent more than 2 years in isolation. [85]

70% of those surveyed by Black and Pink reported
experiencing "emotional pain" from hiding their
sexuality during their incarceration.[86]

Disability and Prison

People in prison are 3x more likely than people outside of prison to have at least one disability.[87]

People categorized as disabled are disproportionately incarcerated. For example, nearly 4 in 10 state prisoners and 3 in 10 federal prisoners reported having a disability; 50% of female state prisoners and 39% of male state prisoners reported having a disability. **The Bureau of Justice Statistics reported that fully 1 in 5 people in prison have a serious mental illness.**[88]

The high rate of incarceration of people with disabilities is largely a result of the closure of facilities that previously housed people with mental health issues. In 1955, state mental health institutions held 559,000 people in the US—roughly the same population as prisons. By 2000, it had fallen to less than 100,000—about 7% of the prison population at that time.[89]

These problems are particularly evident in jails, which typically have even fewer services than prisons. According to research by the Oregon Criminal Justice Commission, "Jails have become the default case management system for repeat, low-level offenders who are often houseless, often have substance abuse disorders, and often have mental health issues, traumatic brain injuries, or other chronic health issues."[90]

People with disabilities are subject to greater abuse and mistreatment in prison.

A report by the Center for American Progress noted that in 4 out of 12 of the California prisons studied, **84 to 94% of all incidents of state use of force were directed towards inmates with cognitive disabilities.**[91]

In Colorado, individuals with cognitive disabilities were 10 times more likely to have the state use force against them than those without. Incarcerated individuals with cognitive disabilities also experience a higher prevalence of sexual assault.[92]

And the impact of incarceration on mental health can be long term. As a team of psychiatrists from the University of Pennsylvania concluded, "Incarceration is related to subsequent mood disorders, related to feeling 'down,' including major depressive disorder, bipolar disorder, and dysthymia. These disorders, in turn, are strongly related to disability, more strongly than substance abuse disorders and impulse control disorders."[93]

"Once I saw I couldn't get a pusher I gave up. If I want to go to rec to play chess, I might have to go [to] the restroom. **It's mind-wrecking when I can't go.** I have to urinate or whatever on myself and I'm tired of that so I just stay in because I can't get nobody to stay with me or assist me."[94]

HARRELL BONNER

incarcerated in New York,
wheelchair user

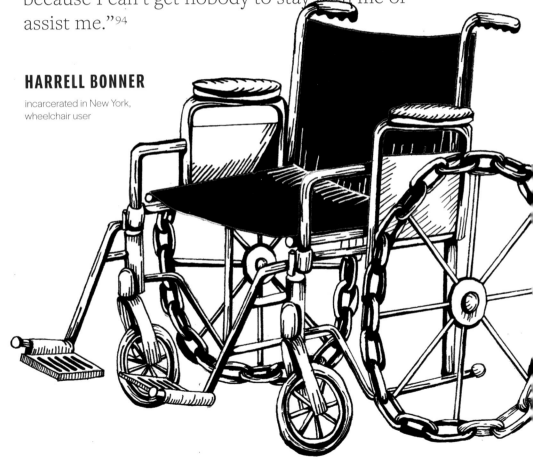

People with disabilities are denied accommodations in prison and jail.

Many prisons implement the dehumanizing practice of placing people with disabilities in solitary confinement, simply because they have no idea what to do with them.

1. Lack of screening, academic accommodations, or social accommodations for people with cognitive disabilities or who are neurodivergent

The lack of screening or up-to-date screening of people arriving in prison with cognitive disabilities means that many people, especially people of color, go undiagnosed, and therefore do not receive the accommodations they need. Furthermore, there is a lack of social or academic accommodations for neurodivergent people, which often leads to social exploitation, higher rates of sexual abuse, much higher rates of violence from prison guards, and a lack of access to programs that could reduce their time. This is painfully represented in the education requirements for release or parole.

25% of state prisoners reported a cognitive disability;

12% reported an ambulatory disability;

12% reported a vision disability;

10% reported a hearing disability.[95]

2. Lack of wheelchairs or wheelchair accessibility, crutches, walkers, or canes

The lack of wheelchairs or wheelchair accessibility for people who are wheelchair dependent is inhumane. Robert Dinkins reported that when he was in solitary confinement, his wheelchair was confiscated, forcing him to crawl around on the ground.[96]

3. Lack of hearing aids, videophones, or sign language interpreters

Prisons often lack videophones, which are the most commonly used technology for deaf people to call each other. The existing technology in prisons tends to be either broken or unusable, leaving deaf people cut off from their family and friends.[97] The lack of availability of hearing aids or sign language interpreters means that incarcerated people who are hard of hearing or deaf can become extremely isolated and unable to access programs, and sometimes they are even punished for their inability to obey orders they cannot hear.

"Mass incarceration of people with disabilities is unjust, unethical, and cruel. But it is also penny-wise and pound-foolish, as community-based treatment and prevention services cost far less than housing an individual behind bars."[98]

REBECCA VALLAS

Youth Justice

In 1995, after nearly two decades of mass incarceration, the US reached its peak level of juvenile incarceration, with more than 380,000 people under the age of 18 locked up. This was intensified by the policy of most states to try many juveniles as adults. This practice began in Florida in 1978 but spread to all states in the 1990s. The increase in the arrests of youth was also related to the increasing presence of police, titled as school resource officers, on high school campuses, especially in schools with a high presence of Black and Brown students. Many people labeled the funneling of youth into incarceration "the school-to-prison pipeline."

By the mid-1990s, a shift in consciousness occurred, and the majority of states began to roll back the prosecution of juveniles. Many states closed state youth prisons. As a result, the incarcerated youth population fell by 70% from 1995 to 2019. But this did not eradicate all the problems with the juvenile justice system. Racial disparity remained, with Black youth more than 4 times as likely to be jailed as white youth and Indigenous youth about 3 times as likely.[99] Furthermore, in some places youth incarceration was ridden with scandals. In one of the most infamous, the 2003–2008 Cash for Kids case in Luzerne County, Pennsylvania, two judges received thousands of dollars from for-profit youth jails for sentencing youth to those institutions. The two judges, Michael Conahan and Mark Ciavarella, were charged and found guilty. Conahan got a 17-year sentence; Ciavarella received 28 years.[100]

What Juvenile Detention Looks Like

For the most part, juvenile sentences average much shorter than those of adults. Two-thirds of youth are held between 1 month and 6 months, and about ¼ are held for between 6 and 12 months.[101]

Crucially, about 1 in 10 youth are held in adult jails and prisons, which puts them at risk and also means that they often cannot access the services they need.

One in 5 kids in juvenile prisons and jails have not been found guilty or delinquent and are awaiting trial.

Marginalized populations are disproportionately targeted.

In 2015, 1 in 5 detained youth were LGBTQ+, meaning that LGBTQ+ youth were twice as likely to be detained. In detention centers and correctional settings,

**Artwork by S., a youth
incarcerated in Montana**
Quaranzine #2, Free Verse

You may feel anger and Pain but remember it will
end for you just keep your head up
and stay strong

Honey-bunning
Corrections officers at the Miami-Dade Regional Juvenile Detention Center bribed incarcerated juveniles with honey buns and other food to savagely assault each other.[108]

LGBTQ+ youth also report being sexually assaulted at a rate of 7 times higher than straight youth.[102]

Furthermore, youth of color are more likely to be detained before trial or adjudication than white youth, which can drastically affect their sentencing outcome.[103]

Long-Term Impact of Juvenile Incarceration

Incarceration impacts youth greatly, even in situations of temporary detention pretrial. This pretrial detention increases the chances that youth will be found guilty and sentenced.

Incarceration and detention disrupts the academic pathways of youth and makes it less likely that youth will finish school.[104]

Over 47% of youth in custody did not have access to GED preparation, job training, college coursework, or GED testing.[105]

Progress Is Underway

For those juveniles not propelled directly into the adult court system, most jurisdictions have a system that holds people under 18 in a juvenile prison. By 2000, juvenile prisons and detention facilities held over 100,000 people. However, unlike in the adult system, at that point advocates for reducing the incarcerated population of youth began to see results from their efforts to reduce the population in these facilities.

Between 2000 and 2017, the number of people held in juvenile prisons fell by more than 60%. During that period, over 1,200 juvenile facilities closed. This corresponded with a decrease in youth arrests of over 80% from 1996 to 2020. A major factor was that in 2012 a court case, *Miller v. Alabama*, declared that juvenile life without parole was unconstitutional.

A number of factors contributed to these changes: 1) several states raised the age of juvenile court jurisdiction and blocked transfer of youth to adult courts; 2) research increasingly revealed that a person's brain doesn't fully mature until age 25, making subjecting youth to the same punishment as adults seem more irrational; 3) several states eliminated sending juveniles to secure facilities for low-level or nonviolent offenses; 4) a growing recognition that most youth involved in the juvenile justice system have experienced unrecognized and untreated trauma that is only made worse by incarceration.

However, this decline in juvenile incarceration in general also accompanies an increase in the racial injustice and disparity of juvenile incarceration. For example, in 2017, more than 17,500 Black youths were incarcerated compared to 14,000 white youths, even though Black people make up only 13% of the US population. For comparison, there were more white youths incarcerated than Black youths about 20 years ago.[106]

In May 2020, during the increase in release due to COVID-19, detention centers were releasing white youth at a rate 17% higher than Black youth. Furthermore, while the detention of white youth is at an all-time historical low, the detention rates of Black and Latinx youth have risen slightly, resulting in an increase in racial inequality.[107]

Even today, Black kids are still detained at 6.3 times the rate of white kids, and committed at 3.6 times the rate of white kids.[109]

National Center for Juvenile Justice, 2022

OVER 30,000 PEOPLE

PARTICIPATED IN THE PELICAN BAY HUNGER STRIKES.

Resistance

In recent years, resistance to mass incarceration has greatly expanded. Resistance has taken many forms: militant hunger strikes inside maximum-security institutions, campaigns to close prisons and jails or stop the building of new institutions, and popular mobilization focused on issues like New Jim Crow policies and harsh sentencing. People have also fought back through cultural activities, producing murals, music, and poetry and creating prison newspapers. Leadership of this resistance has often included currently incarcerated and formerly incarcerated individuals, but students, academics, faith-based institutions, elected officials, and community members have also taken part.

Men raising fists during the Attica prison uprising
On September 9, 1971, 1,281 incarcerated people in Attica prison rioted and took control of the facility to fight for humane treatment. Forty-three people died, including 33 incarcerated people and 10 correctional officers. All but one were killed by the gunfire of the state police crackdown.
New York State Archives, Division of State Police, September 1971

Pelican Bay Hunger Strikes

The most well-known prison hunger strikes of this era took place at the Pelican Bay State Prison in California. The focal point of the strikes was the Security Housing Unit (SHU), where people were held in solitary confinement for decades, often due to false accusations of gang affiliation.

In 2006, officers at Pelican Bay reorganized the SHU and created the Short Corridor. They placed the most senior leaders of each gang in this unit in hopes of separating them from the other members of their gangs. The officers believed that the rival gang members would never talk to each other.

After years of living in isolation in the same pod, Todd Ashker, Sitawa Jamaa, Arturo Castellanos, and Antonio Guillen overcame their long-held gang hostility to form an alliance. From solitary, 4 men coordinated a prison-wide nonviolent hunger strike against the conditions of solitary confinement.

"Mr. Ashker's outdoors time is in a small, concrete enclosed dog-like yard 1½ hours a day with no exercise equipment other than a hand-ball recently given to the SHU inmates as a result of a hunger strike.

"He claims his yard time is always cancelled due to 'staff training,' and from the years 1989–2011 he received zero time outside, other than when he was allowed to go to into a small enclosed concrete yard. **He spent <u>24 hours a day 7 days a week in a small concrete cell for 22 years.</u>**

"Mr. Ashker's meals are under-portioned, watered down, under-cooked food is spoiled, cold, no nutrition, salad is rotten, trays are always dirty and covered with dirty dish water."[110]

URGENT PETITION TO UN WORKING GROUP ON ARBITRARY DETENTION

submitted by the Center for Human Rights and Constitutional Law

Cruel and unusual dollar at Pelican Bay SHU
An unknown imprisoned artist in the Pelican Bay SHU

Their demands included: to end group punishment and administrative abuse, to abolish the debriefing policy (the practice in California prisons of placing alleged members of gangs in solitary indefinitely until they either died or identified other gang members), to end long-term solitary confinement, to end the denial of food as punishment, and to expand constructive programming for people given indeterminate sentences in the SHU.

The first hunger strike began on July 1, 2011. At its peak, more than 6,500 people from prisons across California refused to eat their meals. The strike lasted until July 20, when the California prison authorities agreed to review the conditions of solitary confinement. The second hunger strike took place from September 26 to October 16, 2011. On its third day, the strike reached its peak of 4,252 people refusing to eat across 8 prisons.[111]

The Short Corridor Collective, as they were now being called, spread word to people across California through letters to friends and families as well as to an activist group.

The third hunger strike began on July 8, 2013. On the first day, over 30,000 people in prisons across California and 4 out-of-state prisons refused their meals. After 3 days, more than 11,000 were still starving themselves. After 50 days, 42 people still had not eaten.[112] **It was the biggest organized hunger strike in US history.**

In the year following, the strike won a victory when more than half of those held in Pelican Bay SHU were transferred to other prisons. A lawsuit filed by the men in Pelican Bay SHU ruled that many of the practices in the SHU violated the constitutional rights of incarcerated people.[113]

By Rashid Johnson, incarcerated in Virginia

Dolores Canales helped start the California Families to Abolish Solitary Confinement in 2013 as a way to support the Pelican Bay hunger strikers. At the time, her son had been in solitary in Pelican Bay for over 12 years, after confidential informants had labeled him a gang member. Canales herself had spent more than two decades in prison, including some time in solitary.

"I feel myself at times as if I'm buried alive, as I feel myself that I wake up in the night

and I can't breathe and I have anxiety, because I just imagine what it's like to be entombed day in and day out in a cement cell like that."[114]

DOLORES CANALES

formerly incarcerated founder of the California Families to Abolish Solitary Confinement, describes what it was like to have her son, John Martinez, in the Pelican Bay SHU for several years
Illustrated by Sean White, currently incarcerated in Texas

The Free Alabama Movement

In 2016, led by the Free Alabama Movement, an organization of individuals inside Alabama prisons, incarcerated people staged the biggest prison strike in US history, involving 24,000 people in 20 states. The organizers labeled the strike as the "Call to Action against Slavery in America." They targeted harsh conditions in prisons, especially the low and in some cases nonexistent wages paid to prison workers. For Melvin Ray (Bennu Hannibal Ra-Sun) and other organizers, this was a continuation of slavery, a practice that was supposed to have ended after the Civil War but has been kept alive by a clause of the 13th Amendment that outlaws slavery "except as a punishment for a crime whereof the party shall have been duly convicted."

"I resist because I have no choice. The rules of prison are made to institutionalize you and make you a slave.

Harriet Tubman spoke about how although she freed hundreds of slaves, she could have freed thousands more if only they knew they were slaves. Well, I know what's going on here, and I reject it wholeheartedly."[115]

MELVIN RAY

(Bennu Hannibal Ra-Sun)
an active member of FAM
*Drawn by William B. Livingston III,
currently incarcerated in Oklahoma*

SHU at St. Clair
Smuggled cell phones have been key to the
movement's ability to show what life inside
the SHU is really like.
Free Alabama Movement YouTube

Prison Innovations

Improvisation and ingenuity can help bring some small human comforts into prison life.

The unforgiving, uniform structure of prison life makes it difficult for a person to hold on to their identity as an individual. In a life of identical clothing, identically bland food, and identical beds and cells, improvising lip stains or a lighter isn't merely about makeup or being able to light a cigarette. Prison innovation serves as a reclamation of control over one's humanity.

The pencil sketches included here were drawn by Angelo, an incarcerated artist. He writes, "If some of what's presented here seems unimpressive, keep in mind that deprivation is a way of life in prison. ... The prison environment is designed and administered for the purpose of suppressing such inventiveness. ... But inmates are resilient if nothing else—what's taken today will be remade by tomorrow, and the cycle goes on and on."[116]

Hole plugged with paper

Screw open to fill or pour

Hardware removed

Salt and pepper shakers
Pencil lead container, empty lip balm, BIC disposable lighter
Pencil diagrams by Angelo, an incarcerated artist, printed in Prisoners' Inventions *(Half Letter Press, 2001; expanded edition, 2020).*

Salt or pepper, or a mix

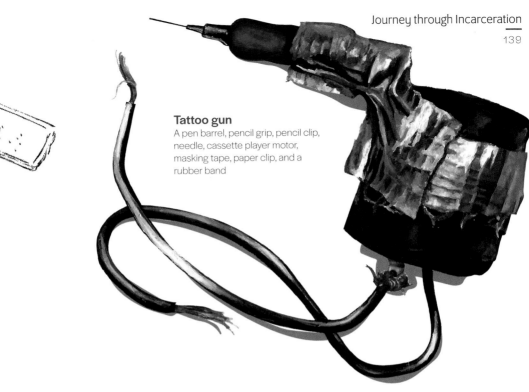

Tattoo gun
A pen barrel, pencil grip, pencil clip, needle, cassette player motor, masking tape, paper clip, and a rubber band

Tattoos

People get tattoos in prison for many reasons. Tattoos can signal what group you belong to and your status in the group. But often, people get tattoos in prison for similar reasons as people get tattoos outside of prison.

"Some people want to look the part, some people actually do get them to illustrate their life story and some probably get them just because it's against the rules to get them done," Dan Grote, a formerly incarcerated prison teacher, said. "Not too different from in the world."[117]

Tattoos of girlfriend's names and wedding bands are just as common as tattoos signaling power or notoriety. They can become a powerful anchor of identity in a system that seeks to erase individuality.

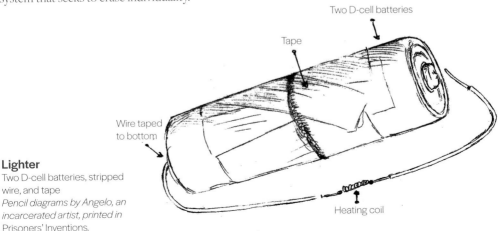

Two D-cell batteries

Tape

Wire taped to bottom

Heating coil

Lighter
Two D-cell batteries, stripped wire, and tape
Pencil diagrams by Angelo, an incarcerated artist, printed in Prisoners' Inventions.

Eyeshadow
Crushed color
pencil lead

Fakeup

Prison restrictions on makeup differ from prison to prison and state to state. Historically, some states, like Virginia, have attempted to ban makeup because of its potential as contraband.

The refusal of prison commissaries to even stock the makeup that is clearly desired by incarcerated people represents a denial of dignity. It is a clear signal by the prisons that the intention of incarceration is not rehabilitation of individuals, but rather retribution and punishment.

It is emotionally difficult and disorienting to be stripped of the tools people rely on to express their identity. While some might find eyeshadow or lipstick frivolous, makeup is an extremely powerful tool for self-identity and sometimes gender affirmation. Prison commissary makeup selection is extremely limited, forcing people to improvise and innovate alternatives to put their self-image together.

Michelle, a woman incarcerated in California, explains, "She gave me colored pencils for my eyeliner, and calamine lotion mixed with coffee grounds for foundation. When your makeup's good and your hair's on point, you feel and act differently; you come to the table stronger because you have your groove on, you're feeling it. It builds up your confidence."[118]

Joyce Pequeño, a 28-year-old woman incarcerated in Oregon, applies makeup every day in prison. She explains, "It makes me feel good, like a real human being—not just a number."[119]

Chess pieces
Toilet paper and water
Pencil diagrams by Angelo,
an incarcerated artist, printed in
Prisoners' Inventions.

Chess

Angelo's former celly (cellmate), Ron, made papier-mâché chess pieces. He "turned out exquisite sets just as fast as the cops could confiscate them. Each set became more elaborate and beautiful—his reasoning being: 'It's the cops' job to keep us down, and ours to show them that they can't.'"[120]

During COVID, social-distancing measures not only forced incarcerated people to often spend 23 hours a day in their cells, but also resulted in the ban of board games, allegedly in the effort to reduce contagion. Harlin Pierce, incarcerated in Texas, and his friend Wally were forced to once again innovate how they played chess in order to maintain their sanity. They began playing chess entirely mentally, without the game board or pieces at all, by shouting the moves of each piece to the grid location, playing the game across the cells and entirely in their minds. In order to make sure they were heard correctly over the din of prison, they created their own phonetic alphabet, shouting, "Bishop to Dinosaur 4" and "Knight captures on Elephant 7!"

As Harlin explained, "While we have been forced to relinquish our physical freedom, we don't have to give up control over our minds."[121]

Lip stain
A bit of hot water
and red M&M's

Cultural Resistance
Making Art in Prison

People in prison use several art forms to both protest prison conditions and maintain a solid state of mind. In virtually every prison and jail in the US, people are using whatever resources available to them to create works of art. Many people use pencils or colored pens to make portraits of themselves or people in their cell block or to design birthday or holiday cards for loved ones. Another common art form involves using wastepaper, especially empty potato chip wrappers, to fashion picture frames, baskets, or handbags. Bar soap can become the medium for shaping chess pieces.

In recent years, social justice activists have created or supported arts programs in many prisons across the country. The Justice Arts Coalition (JAC) brings together many of these programs with the aim of amplifying the voices of incarcerated artists. The JAC works with groups and individuals who are involved in creative writing, poetry, dance, drama, and music. Many of the portraits included in this book have come from artists who are connected to JAC programs.

Apart from graphic arts, thousands of people take to writing while in prison. Many famous prison memoirs have had a huge impact on public consciousness about incarceration. George Jackson's *Soledad Brother* was a bestseller even though the author wrote it while incarcerated and was killed by prison guards before the book was actually published in 1970. Wilbert Rideau wrote of his Louisiana prison experience in the bestseller *In the Place of Justice*. Piper Kerman chronicled her prison year in *Orange Is the New Black*, which became a highly popular TV program. But most prison writers do not become famous. They share their writings with loved ones and hone their craft in isolation.

Fish house
Carole Alden crocheted this fish-shaped tiny house while incarcerated to show her family her plan for where she would live after she got released.
Utah Division of Arts and Museums

In recent years, writing groups inside prisons and jails, such as the Minnesota Prison Writing Workshop, the Michigan Creative Arts Project, Illinois's Prison Neighborhood Arts Project, and the PEN Prison Writing Workshop, have provided mentorship, often from professional writers and instructors, to incarcerated writers. A prison writing group in Connecticut run by author Wally Lamb published two collections of essays that received critical acclaim.

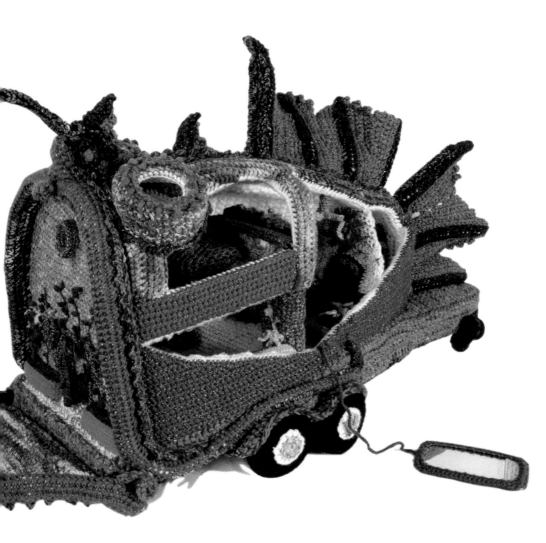

Producing Newspapers in Prison

The first prison newspaper, called the *Forlorn Hope*, hit the presses in 1800 in New York. The pinnacle of prison newspapers was the 1930s to 1950s, when rehabilitation was the dominant paradigm. By 1959, there were 250 prison newspapers. Then came mass incarceration, and the number dwindled to less than a dozen by the early 21st century.

But as awareness of mass incarceration grew, prison newspapers experienced a rebirth. In 2004, people in an Illinois prison, Stateville, launched *Stateville Speaks*, which continued to publish right up until the pandemic. In 2008, *San Quentin News* also resurfaced, and it became the most widely read prison newspaper in the country. The success of prison newspapers has spread to other media. *Ear Hustle*, a podcast produced in San Quentin, has had over 40 million downloads.

Miguel Quezada, a former managing editor at the *San Quentin News*, didn't realize he was a "juvenile lifer," a person sentenced to life for an offense committed when they were under 18, until he was researching a story on juvenile justice for the paper. Ultimately, Quezada got his sentence shortened. He paroled in 2018 and became an active advocate for criminal justice transformation and the release of people serving life sentences for offenses committed when they were under 18.[122]

"It is important for incarcerated people to have a writing outlet, because the system is designed to silence us. Writing is often the only way we can speak. People should read the stories, because we are the forgotten population."

DOROTHY MARAGLINO

incarcerated writer who, among other things, has written about the experience of being raped in prison

"We are reporting behind enemy lines and constantly writing things they don't want us to.

We are always being called liars and being questioned. [Prison administrators] never are. We always have to show proof and they don't."[123]

CHRISTOPHER BLACKWELL
incarcerated in Washington State

Prison Profiteers

US mass incarceration is worth approximately
$182 billion annually.

The era of mass incarceration has seen the enormous expansion of corporate involvement in the world of prisons, jails, pretrial justice, parole, and probation. Historically, prisons and the services tied to the prison industry have been under the authority of the state. The workers in the prison-industrial complex, whether it be wardens, guards, cooks, or admin personnel, were almost all state employees.

However, mass incarceration arose in the era of neoliberalism—the time when government policies and budgets promoted the expansion of the private sector.

Likely the most high-profile corporate players in the prison industry are the private prison operators. Two companies dominate the private prison sector: the GEO Group and CoreCivic. These two companies have similar profiles: not only do they own prisons but they also have interests in immigration detention centers, private probation and parole programs, electronic monitoring, and other services. The GEO Group has shown remarkable growth. From 2001 to 2021, their annual revenue grew from $560 million to $2.25 billion. CoreCivic showed a similar pattern, expanding from $900 million in 2001 to $1.85 billion in 2021.

Yet for all the attention paid to private prisons, they only own or operate about 8% of the prison beds in the US. The remainder are run by state authorities. The number of people held in private prisons increased by only 14% from 2000 to

US government spending
on incarceration surpassed
$89 billion in 2012.[124]

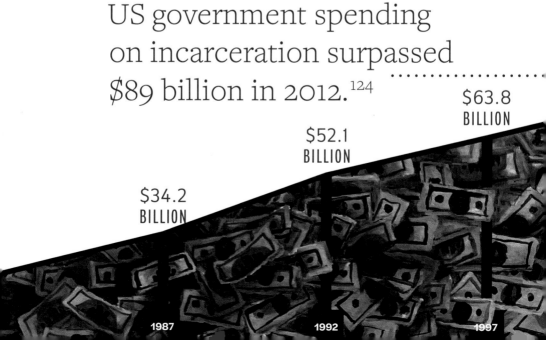

$34.2
BILLION

$52.1
BILLION

$63.8
BILLION

1987   1992   1997

2020. They are of marginal importance in the overall picture. The use of private prisons varies greatly from state to state. Twenty-two states have no private prisons, while Montana holds half of its prison population in private prisons and New Mexico holds 45% in a for-profit institution.[125]

While the GEO Group and CoreCivic are the largest players in the private prison market, other lesser players such as Management and Training Corporation and LaSalle Corrections also operate in this sector.

Private Prisons and Immigration

While private companies have marginal holdings in the criminal legal system, they are major players in immigration detention. They operate about 80% of immigration prison beds, which supplied a little over a quarter of the companies' revenue in 2020. In states like Louisiana and Texas, the state authorities closed private prisons, which the companies then refilled with immigrants.[126]

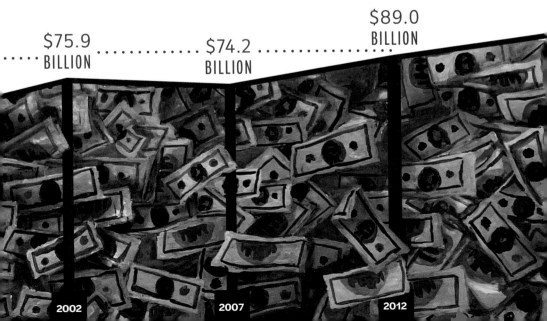

$75.9 BILLION · · · · · · · · · · · $74.2 BILLION · · · · · · · · · · · $89.0 BILLION

2002   2007   2012

Private Sector Players

According to the nonprofit organization Worth Rises, there are over 4,000 corporations that profit from investing in incarceration. One of the biggest sources of profit is food.

In most prisons, a team of incarcerated people assigned to work in the kitchen prepare the meals. Though expenditures may vary, prisons typically spend a little over a dollar per person per meal on food. While no longer consisting of bread and water as in medieval times, the prison diet generally has low nutrition value. Prison food is about cutting costs. Fresh fruit and vegetables are rare, and use of soy meat substitutes is common. Nutraloaf, also known as lockup loaf or punishment loaf, shows up in many prison chow halls. This concoction, composed of a variety of ingredients, has been the subject of lawsuits in at least 6 states, in which litigants declared it cruel and unusual punishment. A Washington court ruled that nutraloaf was punishment, though not cruel and unusual.

In some prisons, private companies run the kitchen, providing both the food and the workforce. Aramark possesses 38% of the market share of the prison food industry.[127] It has been providing food service to prisons since 1976 and currently provides food to more than 500 prisons and jails. Aramark was a primary target in 2017 of hunger strikers in Alabama prisons. There was documented evidence and numerous complaints from incarcerated people of being served rotten meat, food infested with maggots, food that had been nibbled by rats, and food pulled from the trash.[128]

In response to Aramark's association with prisons and a number of legal actions brought against them by incarcerated people, students in many colleges where Aramark provides food service have protested against their universities' contract with the company. Several universities, including New York University, Kent State, and the University of Mississippi, severed their contracts with Aramark.[129]

75% of survey respondents said they were served rotten or spoiled food while they were incarcerated.[130]

Nutraloaf
"The Loaf" is often given to imprisoned people who misbehave day after day. Prisons are allowed to come up with their own version, so these bland loaves can contain anything from leftovers to shredded vegetables.
Wikipedia Commons

Prison Phones

Prison phone calls have been a major source of profits for private companies like Securus and GTL. This is a sector where the shift from public operation to private providers has been very costly to incarcerated people and their loved ones. These companies have been the target of national and state-level campaigns to eliminate excessive tariffs on phone calls from people in prison to their loved ones on the outside. Before the Campaign for Prison Phone Justice put an end to some of this overcharging, people in certain prisons were paying as much as $15 for a 15-minute phone call. Moreover, the contracts between the companies and the Department of Corrections contained kickbacks, meaning that a certain percentage of the revenue from phone calls would be given back to the prisons. In the state of Illinois, 85% of that revenue went to kickbacks.

Through a national campaign that involved incarcerated people and their loved ones, the price of phone calls decreased dramatically in many states and the federal system. In Illinois, the cost of a phone call went from a dollar a minute to a penny a minute, thanks to state legislation driven by activists and engaged legislators.

Nonetheless, companies in many states continue to overcharge. In 2020, the average cost of a 15-minute phone call was $5.74. The total revenue for the prison telecom industry was $1.4 billion. [131]

It would take 11 hours of working at the average maximum wage for a nonindustry job in prison to pay for a 15-minute phone call.

JPay charges 47¢ for each email. That's 5 hours of prison wages.[132]

Securus: Carceral Conglomerate

Securus can be called a "carceral conglomerate," meaning that they have a number of holdings in the prison-industrial complex. Not only do they provide prison phone systems, they also supply video visitation equipment, email systems for prisons and jails, and data management systems for departments of corrections. They also provide tablet devices to over 100,000 incarcerated people and sell content for those devices. They claim to serve over 3,400 "correctional facilities" across the US. Outside of prisons, they are the owners of Satellite Tracking of People, one of the largest providers of electronic monitoring devices in the US. In 2015, Securus bought JPay, an online platform for people to pay bills and fines to departments of corrections, law enforcement, and other prison profiteers. As of 2022, Securus was owned by the private equity firm Platinum Equity.

Securus is often accused of charging exorbitant fees in order to increase profits at the expense of incarcerated people. Until November 2019, Securus sold incarcerated people books at high prices that they obtained freely from Project Gutenberg.[133]

"JPay knows that we are a captive consumer base ... [and] have no choice."[134]

ROGER
incarcerated in New York for 15 years

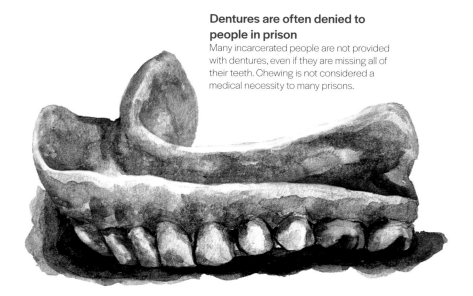

Dentures are often denied to people in prison
Many incarcerated people are not provided with dentures, even if they are missing all of their teeth. Chewing is not considered a medical necessity to many prisons.

Health Care: Merchants of Death

The neoliberal era has featured the privatization of health care in prisons. Companies like Corizon, Wexford, Naphcare, and Wellpath have replaced state-run services across the country, in both prisons and jails. In many places, privatization has come with copays, meaning that incarcerated people, even if they have little or no income, have to pay a fee to see a medical staff person.

Privatized prison health care often leads to an abysmal decline in care. Multiple sources report instances of failure to diagnose treatable illnesses, often resulting in long-term impact and sometimes death, as well as horrifying stories of neglect to the point of cruelty. Research by Reuters into the quality of care by private providers has shown that in many instances, results are problematic. A review of deaths in more than 500 jails from 2016 to 2018 found that the facilities that relied on a private health care provider had death rates 18 to 58% higher than jails where the sheriff's office or local public health departments was the provider. Because the only form of redress available to incarcerated people and their family is through the court, these issues have led to frequent lawsuits. Corizon was sued over 1,300 times between 2011 and 2016.[135]

Notice of impending death
Walter Jordan submitted this letter announcing his impending death under the inadequate medical care of Arizona's Department of Corrections to the court case of *Parsons v. Ryan*. His death 8 days later was deemed likely preventable by expert witness Dr. Todd Wilcox. [137]

"Doctors, NPs, and nurses repeatedly and over many months abdicated their responsibility to care for a sick and dying patient and permitted him to die in pain."[136]

DR. TODD WILCOX

testifying as the expert witness in the court case of *Parsons v. Ryan*, which the ACLU brought against the Arizona Department of Corrections, Rehabilitation, and Reentry (ADCRR) regarding the medical care provided to incarcerated people under its contract with Corizon

P.O BOX 5000
FLORENCe Az 85132

Case 2:12-cv-00601-DKD   Document 2262   Filed 08/29/17   Page 1 of 1

WALTeR JoRdaN
078789

✓ FILED ___ LODGED	
___ RECEIVED ___ COPY	
AUG 2 9 2017	
CLERK U S DISTRICT COURT	
DISTRICT OF ARIZONA	
BY ___ DEPUTY	

United States DisTRict Courts
DisTRict of ARiZONa

ViGtoR PaRsoNs

VS

ChaRles RyaN

NO: CiVl2-0601 DKD

Notice of
IMpeNdiNg Death

ADOC ANd CoRizoN Delayed
TReotiNg My CaNceR. Now because of there
Delay, I May be luckey to be alive foR 30 Days.
The delayed treatMent they gave Me is causing
MeMoRy loss, PaiN. Too MaNy iNMates iN EASt
UNit have the saMe issue (WitheRs, JeNseN,
FigueRoa, TRipati, ORtiz, ThRasheR, RichaRds
etC. ALL these aRe iNMates deNied treatMent
by CoRizoN AMoNg otheRs aNd all falliNg, yelliNg,
SCReaMiNg of PaiN,

WalteR JoRdaN
078789

Prison Labor

Across the USA, incarcerated workers produce more than $2 billion a year in goods and over $9 billion a year in maintenance of the prisons where they are held.[138] **Because of the 13th Amendment, incarcerated people have no right to refuse or choose what labor they are forced to do.** Over 76% of incarcerated workers report that they are not able to refuse working and, if they do so, can be punished with solitary confinement, loss of visitation rights, or loss of opportunities to reduce the length of their sentence, or must work in order to afford basic necessities.[139]

Though much public focus is on the use of prison labor by private companies, in reality, these nonindustry jobs are in the minority, with only about 6,000 people in prisons under any kind of contract to private companies. The majority of incarcerated labor occurs within the prison industry. In most institutions, the incarcerated population is responsible for the day-to-day operations. They cook, clean, serve meals, do paperwork for admin, and carry out the basic maintenance such as plumbing, painting, and building repair. The pay rates for this work range from no pay at all in states like Texas to a few cents an hour in California.

Slavery, Labor, and the 13th Amendment

Many incarcerated people and activists have targeted the 13th Amendment as a farcical initiative. Technically it was supposed to end slavery, but the wording of the amendment, which states, "Neither slavery nor involuntary servitude, except as a punishment for crime whereof the party shall have been duly convicted, shall exist within the United States, or any place subject to their jurisdiction," clearly allows for the use of people in prison as enslaved labor. In 2022, 5 states added a measure on the ballot to eliminate that slavery clause. The measure passed in 4 states: Alabama, Tennessee, Vermont, and Oregon. Louisiana voters rejected the change. Nebraska, Utah, and Colorado had previously passed such legislation.

Apart from the major services mentioned here, over 3,100 companies extract profits from various sources related to prisons and jails.[140] Some of these include: **bail bond companies** (which collect $1.4 billion in nonrefundable fees

every year),[141] **prison commissary vendors** (which infamously inflate prices and take advantage of their captive market and pull in $1.6 billion every year),[142] and **companies that collect fees on transferring money to incarcerated people**, which historically could be performed with mailing a money order. In 2014, JPay collected an average fee of 10% for money transfers, earning a revenue of $53 million.[143]

An incarcerated worker earns on average between 14¢ and 63¢ each hour at 94% of prison jobs.[144]

How Big House Products makes boxer shorts
Pennsylvania Correctional Industries forces incarcerated people to make boxers for little pay. These boxers are then sold back to them through the prison commissary.
James Yaya Hough, incarcerated in PA

Big House Products
Made By
Inmates at
SCI Huntingdon
Cotton/Poly
Blend
Warm Wash
Tumble Dry
BOXER SHORT
X-Large

PART 3

DISMANTLING THE SYSTEM AND BUILDING ANEW

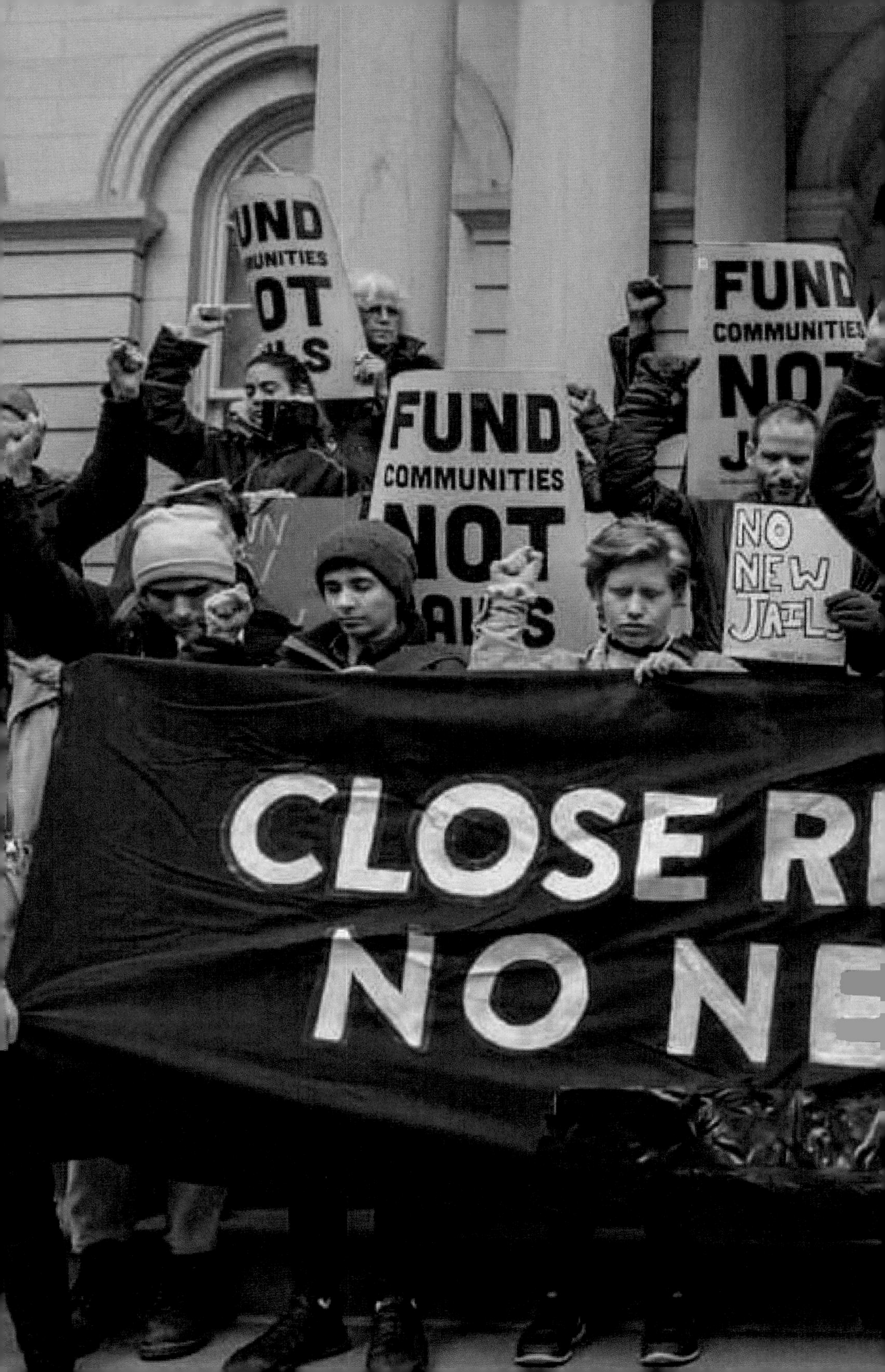
FUND
COMMUNITIES
NOT
FUND
COMMUNITIES
NO
NEW
JAILS

The movement against mass incarceration

In the past decade, political awareness about the excessive use of incarceration in the US has grown exponentially. People have come together in hundreds of organizations and campaigns to try to bring about change.

This work has taken many forms:

Efforts to change sentencing laws, especially those related to drugs

Attempts to halt the building of new prisons and jails or close existing facilities

Lawsuits against inhumane treatment of people who are incarcerated

Campaigns to reduce the charges on prison phone calls or for goods in the commissaries

Mobilizations by formerly incarcerated people to transform the system

Previous Spread:
No New Jails protests
NYC Mayor Bill De Blasio's
plan to open 4 new jails.

Reducing the Prison Population

The number of people incarcerated in the US peaked in 2009 at around 2.4 million. Between that peak and 2019, this figure declined by 11%. All but 4 states reduced their prison population during that time, but for 25 states the reduction was less than 10%. While this seems significant, at this rate it would take 57 years to cut the US prison population in half. This would still leave the US with a higher per capita rate of incarceration than the current rate of any European country.[145]

Several factors led to this decline in prison population: sentencing reform reduced the penalty for certain offenses and created mechanisms for people behind bars to gain early release, and the decriminalization of marijuana in many states also contributed to less people behind bars. These and other changes have been the product of advocacy and mobilization by elected officials, nonprofit organizations, and faith-based groups and the initiative of organizations led by formerly incarcerated people.

The replacement of incarceration by programs that administer less severe punishment than jail or prison has contributed to reducing the number of people behind bars. For example, many jurisdictions have set up drug courts where individuals charged with drug offenses are mandated to go to drug treatment programs rather than jails or prisons.

The relaxation of regulations for parole and supervised release also slowed down the revolving door that sent many people back to prison. In many states, the length of parole terms has been shortened or the penalty for "technical" violations of the rules, like missing a meeting with a parole officer or coming home after curfew, has been moderated, reducing the number of people sent back to prison simply for breaking the often irrational rules that govern parole and probation.

Where is this happening?

The reductions in prison and jail populations have not been uniform. Nearly a third of the population reductions between 2010 and 2020 took place in 2 states: New York and California. Each of these states reduced their prison populations by over 25%. These reductions came about primarily by reductions in penalties for drug offenses and cutbacks for violations of parole regulations. California's reduction was also accelerated by a federal intervention targeted at reducing the overcrowding in a system that was at over 200% of capacity, as well as a moderation of the use of three strikes laws.

By contrast, during this period, 5 states increased their total prison population, and 4 states, West Virginia, Alaska, Nebraska, and Arkansas, saw an uptick in their per capita incarceration rate.

The Path of Reform

The increased awareness of mass incarceration and the reduction in prison populations did not occur by accident. Rather, across the country grassroots organizations emerged to lead campaigns for change.

Drug Policy Alliance

The Drug Policy Alliance is a coalition of organizations and individuals that has been active in campaigns around the country and even internationally to legalize and/or decriminalize drugs and end the War on Drugs. As of 2022, they had 12,000 dues-paying members. In over two decades of operation, they have had numerous victories:

Playing a leading role in establishing the first overdose prevention center (OPC) in the US in New York City. OPCs are safe injection sites that supply people with clean needles and supervision in case of a medical emergency. There are over 200 OPCs worldwide.

Spearheading campaigns to change drug laws, including the decriminalization of marijuana in 26 states plus the District of Columbia. In 2020, the DPA played a major part in backing the campaign in Oregon that passed Measure 110, the first measure that decriminalized all drugs in a state.

The DPA has also advocated for lower budgets for policing the War on Drugs, for the elimination of police in schools, and for ending the militarization of police and the use of "no-knock" warrants, which often lead to attacks on innocent people.

"The Drug War is a manifestation of the things that we have failed at. How do we have a conversation about alternatives?"[146]

KASSANDRA FREDERIQUE

executive director, Drug Policy Alliance

"Formerly incarcerated people have provided us with a counter narrative ... that the system wasn't actually working as advertised and that the human cost and the human tolls was beyond anything that had been communicated to us."[147]

MICHELLE ALEXANDER

author of *The New Jim Crow: Mass Incarceration in the Age of Colorblindness*

Organizations of Impacted People

 Formerly Incarcerated Convicted People and Families Movement

Individuals who have experienced incarceration have come together across the country to speak on their own behalf. An important early effort in this regard came from the New York–based Center for NuLeadership, whose founder, Eddie Ellis, wrote a piece for the *New York Times* that rejected the notion of referring to people who had been incarcerated as "convicts," "criminals," or other such dehumanizing terms.

On the West Coast, All of Us or None, founded in Oakland, California, in 2003, brought together formerly incarcerated people in the Bay Area. They kicked off their program by launching the Ban the Box campaign, an effort to exclude any questions about a person's criminal record from job applications. Their efforts have paid off. Today over 33 states and 150 cities have passed ban the box laws or ordinances.

In 2011, All of Us or None joined with other organizations of formerly incarcerated people, such as the Ordinary People's Society (Alabama), Voice of the Experienced (VOTE) (New Orleans), and A New Way of Life (Los Angeles), to form a national organization, the Formerly Incarcerated Convicted People and Families Movement. They united around a 14-point platform to end mass incarceration, halt immigration detention, and establish equality for all people. By 2022, FICPFM had over 50 organizational members from across the country. In every quarter, they advance the notion that impacted people must have a powerful voice and a full restoration of all rights, including the right to vote while incarcerated. They encapsulated this in the slogan "Nothing about us, without us, is for us."

The National Council for Incarcerated and Formerly Incarcerated Women and Girls

Founded by people incarcerated in the women's federal prison in Danbury, Connecticut, in 2010, the council has taken on the mission to "end the incarceration of women and girls." The council blends national campaigns to bring clemency to people locked up in women's prisons with hyperlocal work such as setting up mutual aid programs in impacted communities during the pandemic. In 2022, they launched a basic income grant program, the Community Love Fund, to materially support women harmed by the criminal legal system. The council also builds ties with women incarcerated in other countries and has formal connections with their sisters in 21 countries in Africa, Asia, Europe, Latin America, and Australia.

Florida Rights Restoration Coalition

Up until 2019, anyone with a felony conviction in Florida could not vote. This prevented 1.4 million people from exercising their franchise. The Florida Rights Restoration Coalition, led by Desmond Meade, a formerly incarcerated individual, put forward an amendment to the state constitution to restore "the voting rights of Floridians with felony convictions after they complete all terms of their sentence including parole or probation." The coalition members traveled across the state of Florida and collected more than 760,000 signatures in support of what became known as Amendment 4.

On election night, 64% of voters supported the measure, restoring voting rights to all those with felony convictions who have completed their sentence, except to those convicted of murder or certain sex offenses. However, once Amendment 4 passed, Governor Ron DeSantis undercut its impact by pushing through a clause that compelled all people with felony convictions to pay any money they owed for fines before they could get their votes restored. Advocates of Amendment 4 fought back by fundraising to collect the money to pay off those fines. Michael Bloomberg, a billionaire Republican CEO, contributed $16 million to the fund.

Despite the triumph of Amendment 4, the denial of voting rights to people with a background still persists. Even after the passage of Amendment 4, over 900,000 people in Florida still could not vote due to felony convictions. As of 2022, 4.6 million people still could not vote in the US due to criminal convictions. One in 19 Black people are denied the vote due to their criminal history, 3.5 times higher than the rate for non-Black people. Maine and Vermont are the only states where people in prison can vote.[148]

Research

Our awareness of the criminal legal system has been greatly enhanced by research. A number of think tanks specialize in researching the prison-industrial complex and producing recommendations for change. Among the most important of these are the Sentencing Project, the Vera Institute, and the Brennan Center. Nonprofit, activist organizations have also contributed to this body of work: Critical Resistance, Survived and Punished, Black and Pink, HEARD, and the Community Justice Exchange are a few of the most important.

Each year the Prison Policy Initiative produces a graphic called "The Whole Pie," which depicts the number of people incarcerated in the US and what type of institution they are held in.

Reform vs. Abolition

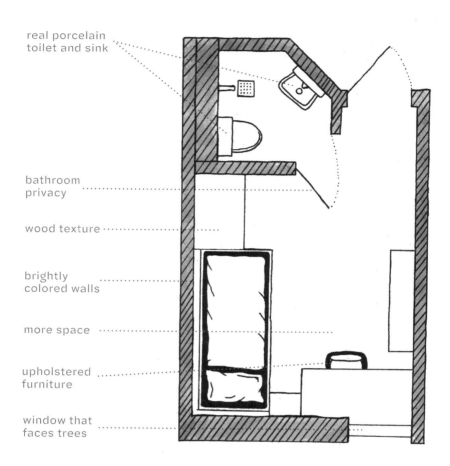

real porcelain
toilet and sink

bathroom
privacy

wood texture

brightly
colored walls

more space

upholstered
furniture

window that
faces trees

The struggle against mass incarceration has sparked great debates about the most effective approach to change the criminal legal system. Some individuals argue that the system is broken and must be fixed. They advocate primarily for **reforms** for reduced sentences, especially for nonviolent offenses, and to improve the conditions of incarceration: improve the food, expand educational opportunities, extend visiting hours. These people are generally referred to as advocates for reforming the criminal justice system.

Other people argue that the entire system must be eliminated, abolished. They reject the notion that the system is broken and therefore must be fixed. Their view, which is referred to as **abolition**, holds that the system is not broken but that it is doing exactly what it was set up to do—enforce and perpetuate a racist, exploitative system.

The Reform View

The reform view contends that when people commit a crime, they should be punished. While criminal justice reformers would argue that the US system is far too punitive, they would hold that some people need to be punished or kept out of circulation. Part of their argument would contend that crimes like murder or rape cannot go unpunished, that victims or survivors of such crimes deserve some kind of justice or satisfaction that the person who committed the crime is paying a price. Their priorities to reform the criminal justice system would include measures like legalizing or decriminalizing substances, offering more programs of rehabilitation in prisons, such as college courses and vocational skills, shortening sentences for nonviolent crimes, and giving people in prison time off their sentences for "good behavior."

Reformers also generally oppose the death penalty, arguing that it is inhumane. Lastly, reformers would generally support measures to address the racial disparities in the criminal legal system, recognizing that race should not be a factor in determining a person's outcome once they enter the court system. All reformers do not think in exactly the same way. Some favor slow-paced change, reducing prison populations by giving people credits for good time while in prison or slightly moderating sentencing laws. Others would opt for much more drastic cuts to prison budgets and much less harsh sentencing, along the lines of many countries in Europe.

Halden Prison yard
While the grounds are beautiful and
covered in trees, the prison wall is visible
everywhere.
North Dakota Legislative Branch

Halden Prison in Norway

Halden Prison in Norway, frequently called the "most humane prison in the world," is often seen as a model for prison reform. Located in a beautifully forested area, Halden has no guard towers or razor wire. Walls are painted in soothing colors and decorated with works of art. People incarcerated there have their own cells with a flat-screen TV, a fridge, and a microwave. Cells are organized in clusters so that each group of cells shares a common kitchen and social space. The prison includes many activities geared toward rehabilitation, from woodworking to a music studio where people can record music and spoken word. The Norwegian government's prison philosophy holds that "the smaller the difference between life inside and outside the prison, the easier the transition from prison to freedom." While this approach has drawn extensive praise from many quarters, a 2021 set of interviews with men incarcerated in Halden revealed that many of them said there was nothing "therapeutic" about the environment of the prison, despite efforts by authorities to create a welcoming atmosphere.

"At Lincoln, the Women's Center for Justice can use a gender-responsive, trauma-informed care model that breaks the cycle of incarceration. It can promote successful reentry by offering a therapeutic setting that fosters community connections, family unification and skills building."

GLORIA STEINEM

in an argument for a proposed women's jail in Harlem

The Abolitionist View

Abolitionists call for the elimination of all prisons and jails. Rather than using a criminal justice framework, most abolitionists refer to acts of violence or other things that would be considered crimes under existing law as harms. The people involved are the harm-doers and the survivors of the harm. They don't believe in using the criminal legal system, or what they often refer to as the criminal punishment system, to address harm.

Rather, they advocate for measures that address the root causes of harm, the elements in the system they call racial capitalism, that propel certain people, especially poor Black and Brown folks, into the prison system. They argue not simply for changes in the criminal legal system but in the entire system of racial capitalism. While they would fight for certain types of reforms, they would argue that the system cannot be reformed piece by piece. In their view, eliminating mass incarceration requires a transformation of society and an end to structural racism.

"Let's begin our abolitionist journey not with the question 'What do we have now and how can we make it better?' Instead, let's ask, 'What can we imagine for ourselves and the world?' If we do that, then boundless possibilities of a more just world await us."[149]

MARIAME KABA

Los Angeles County + USC Medical
Center's Restorative Care Village
The Restorative Care Village aims to provide a
continuum of care, including housing, mental
health resources, substance use disorder
treatment, and transitional aid. The slogan
"Care First, Jail Last" was part of the inspiration
for this $68.5 million facility.
Cannon Design

Abolition as Presence

The most well-known application of the word *abolition* is the abolition of slavery. But to enslaved people, abolition was intimately tied with freedom, with building a new life of prosperity and power. Hence it meant the absence of slavery but also the creation of free families and free communities.

Similarly, the abolition of prisons and jails, while connecting to the absence of these institutions of oppression, is also about a different way of living, creating communities where harm is addressed by making some fundamental changes to the economic, political, and social life of our society.

Abolition aims to address what abolitionists perceive as the root cause of harm: the inequitable distribution of resources and power. Instead of prisons that punish, abolitionists advocate directing resources to programs that keep people out of prison and improve quality of life: guaranteed income, accessible and affordable housing, free and relevant education, improved health care, and measures to ensure the survival of the planet.

"Abolition is about presence, not absence. It has to be green, and in order to be green, it has to be red (anti-capitalist), and in order to be red, it has to be international."

RUTH WILSON GILMORE

The First Step Act

A Case Study in Theories of Change

In 2018, President Donald Trump, largely under the influence of entertainer Kim Kardashian, put forward the First Step Act. Passed in 2018 by a bipartisan vote, the First Step Act was an example of a moderate approach to criminal justice reform. The goal of the First Step Act was sentencing reform, in particular reducing some of the mandatory minimum sentences in the federal system. The act shortened mandatory minimum sentences for nonviolent drug offenses. It also gave judges more discretion to deviate from the mandatory minimum guidelines. One highly publicized component of the First Step Act was to reduce the disproportionate penalties for crack cocaine as opposed to powder cocaine.

The Impact of the First Step Act

After one year, because of the First Step Act, about 2,000 people received sentence reductions for convictions related to crack cocaine; 342 people were approved for early home confinement (house arrest); 107 people received compassionate release; 2,000 people received good time credits that earned them an early release.

In 2019, the federal prison system held just under 180,000 people. Hence, overall just a few thousand were impacted by the First Step Act. Moreover, more than half of those people incarcerated in the federal system have sentences of 10 years or longer. Over a quarter have more than 15 years. Good time credits will have little effect on these individuals' sentences.

Reactions to the First Step Act

Many criminal justice reformers praised the First Step Act. They argued that because it drew support from both Democrats and Republicans, it laid the groundwork for future unity across the aisle for greater change. While not promoting the First Step Act as a panacea for the problems of the system, supporters of the act like the Brennan Center described this as a "critical win in the fight to reduce mass incarceration ... the largest step the federal government has taken to reduce the number of people in federal custody."

A coalition of over 100 organizations signed a letter in opposition to the First Step Act. They argued that while they supported the intention of the act to reduce penalties and prison populations, it made no real change to existing systems. They maintained the First Step Act would not significantly impact racial disparities or excessively long mandatory minimum sentences nor address the lack of rehabilitation in federal prisons. They also decried the failure of the act to reduce the costs of incarceration.

In short, they argued that it was a cosmetic change that didn't address the structure of the criminal legal system or the ways in which federal budgets prioritized prisons and prosecutions over supportive programs like mental health services, housing support, substance use programs, job creation, and postprison education.

AN ABOLITIONIST CHECKLIST FOR THE FIRST STEP ACT

While abolitionists call for the elimination of prisons, they recognize this will not happen overnight. In the meantime, they support certain types of reforms, which they label "nonreformist reforms." In order to determine whether to support a certain reform, abolitionists check to see if the reform:

- [ ] reduces the incarcerated population

- [ ] reduces the powers and budgets of the prison-industrial complex

- [ ] does not aid one sector of the impacted population while deepening the punishment of another sector

- [ ] builds the power of movements fighting for change

Seen through the abolitionist lens, the First Step Act likely would not be labeled a nonreformist reform. The act led to a slight reduction in the incarcerated population but did little to reduce the power or budgets of the federal prison system, nor did it allocate funds to programs or organizations fighting for change.

The Campaign to Close Rikers

A Case Study in Theories of Change

Rikers Island in New York City is one of the biggest jail complexes in the world. The island houses 10 jails with a total capacity of nearly 15,000 people. Over the years, conditions at Rikers have deteriorated. In 2015, the jail recorded 9,424 assaults. In 2016, a group led by individuals who had been incarcerated at Rikers began to press for the closure of the jail complex. This would become the Campaign to Close Rikers, which eventually had over 120 organizations as members. Their mobilizations influenced a 2016 study commissioned by the city that recommended the closure of Rikers within 10 years.

The challenges that arose from the recommendation to close Rikers prompted enormous debates among those who had been trying for years to address the violence and deteriorating physical conditions in the jail. The campaign carried out incessant activities to get their point across. Their actions played an important part in convincing elected officials that it was time to close the jail complex. In October 2019, the city council voted to close the jail by 2026. But the story didn't end there. The key question that emerged was: What next? The debate over the next steps reflected the differences of opinions among the campaigners.

REFORMERS PROPOSED BUILDING A NEW SET OF JAILS

The criminal justice reformers wanted to build a set of new jails to replace the massive Rikers facility. They proposed 4 jails distributed throughout different parts of the city. These jails were to be modern, friendly facilities, situated in the communities where those confined on Rikers came from. According to city authorities, these jails were "to foster safety and wellbeing for both those incarcerated and for staff, providing space for quality education, health, and therapeutic programming. Modern facilities can also serve as a catalyst for positive change in the community and the broader justice system."

Unlike during the years when mass incarceration was unfolding, there was no disagreement about the need for change. There was general agreement that the population of the jail needed to decrease. The issue was, by how much?

There was also general agreement that much of the funding that went to operating the traditional Rikers Island jail should be reallocated. It was estimated that cutting the costs of the jail would save $1.8 billion per year. The question was: Should that money be directed at community investments outside the criminal legal system or should it go to new types of initiatives inside jails, like better mental health services or establishing gender-responsive jails that offer programming and services more in line with the needs of those incarcerated who identify as women, as mothers, as grandmothers?

The debates over Rikers Island are not isolated. They echo through struggles over how to change the realities of mass incarceration and the prison-industrial complex in communities around the country. Whether in the biggest city in the US or in small rural counties, the debate continues among those fighting for change: How far does that change go? What is our ultimate vision for where that change ends up?

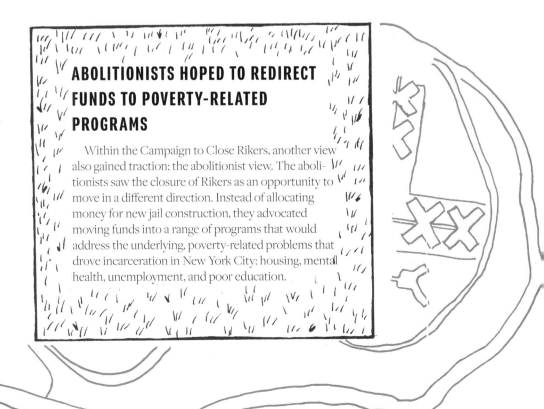

ABOLITIONISTS HOPED TO REDIRECT FUNDS TO POVERTY-RELATED PROGRAMS

Within the Campaign to Close Rikers, another view also gained traction: the abolitionist view. The abolitionists saw the closure of Rikers as an opportunity to move in a different direction. Instead of allocating money for new jail construction, they advocated moving funds into a range of programs that would address the underlying, poverty-related problems that drove incarceration in New York City: housing, mental health, unemployment, and poor education.

Models of Justice

Punishment, revenge, and retribution dominate the US criminal legal system. But recent uprisings against police violence and protests about mass incarceration have inspired activists to reimagine what justice looks like. This has led US organizations and communities to study alternative models such as restorative justice and transformative justice. People in some parts of the world have been using these models for years. Today, grassroots structures in some US communities are following suit and implementing these models to address conflict, violence, harm, and inequity.

Retributive Justice

Retributive justice centers the idea that those who do harm must pay, must face punishment and retribution. This is the foundation of our criminal legal system, which, through the courts, assigns a specific punishment to each offense. This is also the basis of what some refer to as "street justice," or an eye for an eye.

Retributive justice focuses on the past and acts to "rebalance" the scales of justice. There is little emphasis on healing or change, and little involvement of the people who are harmed by the crime, other than delivering testimony.

When retributive justice is carried out by the courts, it is centered on what is legally defined as a crime rather than harm; that is, people are prosecuted for breaking the law, rather than harming another person. Communities are made reliant on the state to answer to crimes committed. Blame is placed on the individual, rather than the larger system. The individual's criminal record becomes a permanent stigma they must shoulder for life.

Restorative Justice

Restorative justice centers the idea that a person who does harm must admit their action to the person, community, or organization they have harmed, show some understanding of the impact of that harm, and take some action to restore or compensate for the harm done. For example, in the case of a person who steals $20 from someone, paying back the $20 could be part of restorative justice. But it might also include asking the person to acknowledge that the theft did harm. Restorative justice becomes more complicated when the harm involves great violence such as a murder and when the criminal legal system is determined to punish the harm-doer.

Crucially, unlike retributive justice, restorative justice strives to help heal the person who was harmed. The person who does harm is also given the ability to repair the harm and is not defined solely by their ability to perpetrate harm. Restorative justice involves rethinking the past in order to avoid harm in the future.

Transformative Justice

Transformative justice centers the idea that harm is often done because of the unjust way that society functions. In transformative justice, we might ask someone to acknowledge that they stole $20, but we may also try to rectify the circumstances that led them to steal that $20, whether it be substance use, unemployment, low wages, or health care costs. Transformative justice promotes healing, safety, and accountability, not punishment.

Groups that practice transformative justice focus on building the power and capacity to prevent harm before it happens. This means challenging political and economic structures while developing grassroots mutual aid, harm reduction, and conflict deescalation programs.

"Transformative Justice is practice. It's brotherhood and sisterhood, it's fatherhood and motherhood—it's family. It's community, it's culture … it's having the courage to attempt to address the ills of this complex society with love, empathy, and compassion."[150]

NYAKO PIPPEN

currently serving life in Florida

Imagine a world without prisons or jails.

The US government spends about $80 billion per year on prisons and jails. In 2018, the national average for school spending per pupil was $12,612. The average cost to keep a person in prison for a year was about $30,000.

This $80 billion could:

Build 1,000 high schools

Construct 320,000 low-income apartments

Pay the salaries of a million nurses

Cover the operating costs of 1.6 million wind turbines

When we look back on the movement to abolish slavery, it seems absurd to think of tinkering with slavery to create a few rules and policies to make for a gentler, kinder enslavement. Yet this is precisely what the dominant thinking is about how we handle prisons and jails.

We can't think about abolishing prisons without also addressing other institutions of violence and punishment. As we reimagine a world without prisons, let us also think about other sources of violence in our society. Think, for example, of the amount of resources that are spent on policing, on the military, and on economic activities that degrade the planet. As we imagine a world without prisons, we must also make connections to other ways that punishment, violence, and profiteering endanger lives and communities and consider what needs to be done to build the power to change this entire system.

"If we are to move into a future, we need to do no less than reimagine what it means to be human in relationship to one another and to the Earth and her inhabitants."[151]

FANIA DAVIS

Notes

1   Wendy Sawyer and Peter Wagner, "Mass Incarceration: The Whole Pie 2022," Prison Policy Initiative, March 14, 2022, https://www.prisonpolicy.org/reports/pie2022.html.

2   E. Ann Carson, "Prisoners in 2019," Bureau of Justice Statistics, US Department of Justice, October 2020, https://bjs.ojp.gov/library/publications/prisoners-2019.

3   Tianna Herring and Emily Widra, "What the Survey of Prison Inmates Tells about Trans People in State Prison," Prison Policy Initiative, March 31, 2022, https://www.prisonpolicy.org/blog/2022/03/31/transgender_incarceration.

4   Laura M. Maruschak, Jennifer Bronson, and Mariel Alper, "Disabilities Reported by Prisoners: Survey of Prison Inmates, 2016," Bureau of Justice Statistics, US Department of Justice, March 2021, https://bjs.ojp.gov/library/publications/disabilities-reported-prisoners-survey-prison-inmates-2016.

5   Maruschak, Bronson, and Alper, "Disabilities Reported by Prisoners."

6   Herring and Widra, "Survey of Prison Inmates."

7   Matthew Green, "Packing the House: The Back Story on California's Prison Boom," KQED, January 6, 2012, https://www.kqed.org/lowdown/457/packing-the-house-how-big-is-californias-prison-system.

8   Peter Wagner and Bernadette Rabuy, "Following the Money of Mass Incarceration," Prison Policy Initiative, January 25, 2017, https://www.prisonpolicy.org/reports/money.html.

9   Benjamin Todd Jealous and Lateefah Simon, "The Root: We Can't Afford Not to Fix Our Justice System," NPR, April 7, 2011, https://www.npr.org/2011/04/07/135203031/the-root-we-cant-afford-to-not-fix-justice-system.

10   Bruce Western, *Punishment and Inequality in America* (New York: R. Sage Foundation, 2006), 175.

11   Angela Davis, "Masked Racism: Reflections on the Prison Industrial Complex," *ColorLines*, September 10, 1998, colorlines.com/article/masked-racism-reflections-prison-industrial-complex.

12   United States v. Lomax, 8:92CR12-2 (2015).

13   "10 Reasons to Oppose '3 Strikes, You're Out,'" ACLU, March 17, 2002, https://www.aclu.org/documents/10-reasons-oppose-3-strikes-youre-out.

14   James Kilgore, *Understanding Mass Incarceration: A People's Guide to the Key Civil Rights Struggle of Our Time* (New York: The New Press, 2015), 116.

15   "Report to the United Nations on Racial Disparities in the U.S. Criminal Justice System," Sentencing Project, April 19, 2018, https://www.sentencingproject.org/reports/report-to-the-united-nations-on-racial-disparities-in-the-u-s-criminal-justice-system.

16   Norman J. Clement et al., "The 'Reel' Reason United States Drug Enforcement Administration (DEA) Was Formed, Thus Explaining the Attack on Black-Owned Pharmacy Businesses (Light)," You Are within the Norms, May 13, 2021, https://youarewithinthenorms.com/2021/05/13/the-reel-reason-united-states-drug-enforcement-administration-dea-was-formed-thus-explaining-the-attack-on-black-owned-pharmacy-businesses-light.

17   Kilgore, *Understanding Mass Incarceration*, 61.

18   Anna King, "The Fog of Pot," *Los Angeles Review of Books*, August 3, 2013, https://
        lareviewofbooks.org/article/the-fog-of-pot.

19   Shannon Mullen, Lisa Robyn Kruse, Andrew J. Goudsward, and Austin Bogues, "Crack
        vs. Heroin: An Unfair System Arrested Millions of Blacks, Urged Compassion for
        Whites," *Asbury Park Press*, December 2, 2019, https://www.app.com/in-depth/
        news/local/public-safety/2019/12/02/crack-heroin-race-arrests-blacks-
        whites/2524961002.

20   Kara Gotsch and Vinay Basti, "Capitalizing on Mass Incarceration: U.S. Growth in
        Private Prisons," Sentencing Project, August 2, 2018, https://www.sentencingproject.
        org/reports/capitalizing-on-mass-incarceration-u-s-growth-in-private-prisons.

21   Daniel Trotta, "Despite Trump's 'Law and Order' Rhetoric, Protestors Won't Back
        Down," Reuters, September 11, 2020, https://www.reuters.com/article/us-global-
        race-usa-protests/despite-trumps-law-and-order-rhetoric-protesters-wont-back-
        down-idUSKBN2621C3.

22   "Forced Apart: Families Separated and Immigrants Harmed by US Deportation Policy,"
        Human Rights Watch, July 17, 2007, https://www.hrw.org/report/2007/07/17/
        forced-apart/families-separated-and-immigrants-harmed-united-states-deportation.

23   "ICE Total Removals through July 31, 2011," Immigration and Customs Enforcement,
        2011, https://www.ice.gov/doclib/about/offices/ero/pdf/ero-removals.pdf.

24   Trotta, "Trump's 'Law and Order' Rhetoric."

25   David J. Bier, "A Wall Is an Impractical and Ineffective Border Plan," Cato Institute,
        November 28, 2016, https://www.cato.org/blog/border-wall-impractical-
        expensive-ineffective-plan.

26   Kilgore, *Understanding Mass Incarceration*, 81.

27   Zhen Zeng and Todd D. Minton, "Jail Inmates in 2019," Bureau of Justice Statistics, US
        Department of Justice, March 2021, https://bjs.ojp.gov/library/publications/
        jail-inmates-2019.

28   Zeng and Minton, "Jail Inmates in 2019."

29   Zhen Zeng and Todd D. Minton, "Jail Inmates in 2020—Statistical Tables," Bureau of
        Justice Statistics, US Department of Justice, December 2021, https://bjs.ojp.gov/
        library/publications/jail-inmates-2020-statistical-tables.

30   "Under Pressure: How Fines and Fees Hurt People, Undermine Public Safety, and
        Drive Alabama's Racial Wealth Divide," Alabama Appleseed Center for Law and
        Justice, 2019, https://alabamaappleseed.org/underpressure.

31   "The Human Toll of Jail," Vera Institute of Justice, 2019, https://www.vera.org/
        the-human-toll-of-jail-2023.

32   Stephanie Wykstra, "Bail Reform, Which Could Save Millions of Unconvicted People
        from Jail, Explained," *Vox*, October 17, 2018, https://www.vox.com/future-
        perfect/2018/10/17/17955306/bail-reform-criminal-justice-inequality.

33   Wendy Sawyer, "How Race Impacts Who Is Detained Pretrial," Prison Policy Initiative,
        October 9, 2019, https://www.prisonpolicy.org/blog/2019/10/09/pretrial_race.

34   Wykstra, "Bail Reform."

35   Sawyer, "How Race Impacts."

36   Alysia Santo, "Bail Reformers Aren't Waiting for Bail Reform," Marshall Project, August
        23, 2016, www.themarshallproject.org/2016/08/23/bail-reformers-aren-t-waiting-for-
        bail-reform.

37   "Data Portal," Measures for Justice, updated January 14, 2022, https://app. measuresforjustice.org/portal.

38   John Annese, "Mom Dies of 'Broken Heart' after Son Kalief Browder Killed Himself Last Year," *New York Daily News*, October 16, 2016, https://www.nydailynews. com/2016/10/16/mom-dies-of-broken-heart-after-son-kalief-browder-killed-himself-last-year.

39   Leonard Greene, "Bronx Streetcorner Renamed 'Kalief Browder Way' on Former Rikers Inmate's 24th Birthday," *New York Daily News*, May 25, 2017, https://www. nydailynews.com/2017/05/25/bronx-streetcorner-renamed-kalief-browder-way-on-former-rikers-inmates-24th-birthday.

40   Ashley Nellis, "No End In Sight: America's Enduring Reliance on Life Sentences," Sentencing Project, February 17, 2021, https://www.sentencingproject.org/reports/ no-end-in-sight-americas-enduring-reliance-on-life-sentences.

41   Alleen Brown, "Trapped in the Floods: With Floodwaters Rising, Prisoners Wait for Help in Floating Feces," *Intercept*, February 12, 2022, https://theintercept. com/2022/02/12/prison-climate-crisis-flood.

42   "24 Hours in Prison," North Carolina Department of Public Safety, accessed November 9, 2023, https://www.doc.state.nc.us/dop/hours24.htm.

43   Renaldo Hudson, "Thank You for My Freedom, Gov. Pritzker, It Is Time to Do More," Illinois Prison Project, March 2021, https://www.illinoisprisonproject.org/stories/ renaldo-hudson.

44   Dan Nolan and Chris Amico, "Solitary by the Numbers," *Frontline*, PBS, April 18, 2017, apps.frontline.org/solitary-by-the-numbers.

45   Alison Shames, Jessa Wilcox, and Ram Subramanian, "Solitary Confinement: Common Misconceptions and Emerging Safe Alternatives," Vera Institute of Justice, May 2015, https://www.vera.org/publications/solitary-confinement-common-misconceptions-and-emerging-safe-alternatives.

46   Ed Pilkington, "Nearly 50,000 People Held in Solitary Confinement in US, Report Says," *Guardian*, August 24, 2022, www.theguardian.com/us-news/2022/aug/24/ us-solitary-confinement-prisons.

47   Judith Resnick, Skylar Albertson, Grace Y. Li, and Jennifer Taylor, "Time-in-Cell: A 2021 Snapshot of Restrictive Housing Based on a Nationwide Survey of U.S. Prison Systems," Yale University Liman Center paper, August 24, 2022, https://dx.doi. org/10.2139/ssrn.4206981.

48   Ronald Clark, "Voices from Solitary: This Inhumane Project Called Solitary Confine-ment," *Solitary Watch*, September 20, 2021, https://solitarywatch.org/author/ voicesfromsolitary.

49   Alysia Santo, "Prison Rape Allegations Are on the Rise," Marshall Project, July 25, 2018, www.themarshallproject.org/2018/07/25/prison-rape-allegations-are-on-the-rise.

50   Derek Gilna, "$60 Million in Strip Search Settlements for Cook County Jail Prisoners," *Prison Legal News*, September 15, 2011, https://www.prisonlegalnews.org/ news/2011/sep/15/60-million-in-strip-search-settlements-for-cook-county-jail-prisoners.

51   Stacy M. Brown, "Senate Committee Finds Widespread Employee on Inmate Sex Abuse in Federal Prisons," *Amsterdam News*, December 26, 2022, https:// amsterdamnews.com/news/2022/12/26/senate-committee-finds-widespread-employee-on-inmate-sex-abuse-in-federal-prisons.

52   E. Ann Carson, "Mortality in Local Jails, 2000–2019—Statistical Tables," Bureau of Justice Statistics, US Department of Justice, December 2021, https://bjs.ojp.gov/library/publications/mortality-local-jails-2000-2019-statistical-tables.

53   Jennifer Bronson and Marcus Berzofsky, "Indicators of Mental Health Problems Reported by Prisoners and Jail Inmates, 2011–2012," Bureau of Justice Statistics, US Department of Justice, June 2017, https://bjs.ojp.gov/library/publications/indicators-mental-health-problems-reported-prisoners-and-jail-inmates-2011.

54   Jeffrey McKee, "Mental Health Services Lacking in Washington Prisons," Prison Journalism Project, May 13, 2022, prisonjournalismproject.org/2022/05/13/mental-health-services-lacking-in-washington-prisons.

55   Laura M. Maruschak, Jennifer Bronson, and Mariel Alper, "Indicators of Mental Health Problems Reported by Prisoners and Jail Inmates, 2016," Bureau of Justice Statistics, US Department of Justice, June 2021, https://bjs.ojp.gov/library/publications/indicators-mental-health-problems-reported-prisoners-survey-prison-inmates.

56   "COVID behind Bars Data Project," UCLA Law, accessed November 9, 2023, uclacovidbehindbars.org.

57   Chuck Sharman, "Antiviral Pills to Fight COVID-19 Sitting Unused in Pharmacies, but Prisoners Go Wanting," *Prison Legal News*, March 9, 2022, https://www.prisonlegalnews.org/news/2022/may/9/antiviral-pills-fight-covid-19-sitting-unused-pharmacies-prisoners-go-wanting.

58   "Prison Policy Initiative COVID-19 Resources," Prison Policy Initiative, April 2023, www.prisonpolicy.org/virus.

59   "What Coronavirus Quarantine Looks Like in Prison," *Life Inside* (blog), Marshall Project, March 18, 2020, https://www.themarshallproject.org/2020/03/18/what-coronavirus-quarantine-looks-like-in-prison.

60   "'It's Basically a Death Sentence': Hunger Strikers Demand Release as Virus Surges in ICE Jails," *Democracy Now!*, transcript, August 4, 2020, https://www.democracynow.org/2020/8/4/ice_jails_hunger_strikes.

61   Sawyer and Wagner, "Mass Incarceration."

62   James Kilgore, *Understanding E-Carceration: Electronic Monitoring, the Surveillance State, and the Future of Mass Incarceration* (New York: The New Press, 2022), 69.

63   Kilgore, *Understanding E-Carceration*, 69.

64   Kilgore, *Understanding E-Carceration*, 69.

65   Lucius Couloute and Daniel Kopf, "Out of Prison, Out of Work: Unemployment among Formerly Incarcerated People," Prison Policy Initiative, July 2018, https://www.prisonpolicy.org/reports/outofwork.html.

66   Couloute and Kopf, "Out of Prison, Out of Work."

67   Christie Thompson, "No Photo ID, No Services: Coronavirus Poses Steep Hurdles after Prison," Marshall Project, May 26, 2020, https://www.themarshallproject.org/2020/05/26/no-photo-id-no-services-coronavirus-poses-steep-hurdles-after-prison.

68   "Driver's License Costs by State, 2018," Ballotpedia, March 2018, https://ballotpedia.org/Driver%27s_license_costs_by_state,_2018.

69   Patrick Smith, "Stable Housing for Former Prisoners Could Save Illinois $100M a Year," WBEZ Chicago, July 31, 2019, https://www.wbez.org/stories/stable-housing-for-former-prisoners-could-save-illinois-100-million-annually/d31aa5b3-075c-4fea-b1cb-2ba0d511236c.

70 "'Repair the Damage from the Drug War': Susan Burton on A New Way of Life to End Mass Incarceration," *Democracy Now!*, transcript, May 19, 2017, https://www.democracynow.org/2017/5/19/repair_the_damage_from_the_drug.

71 E. Ann Carson and William J. Sabol, "Aging of the State Prison Population, 1993–2013," Bureau of Justice Statistics, US Department of Justice, May 2016, https://bjs.ojp.gov/library/publications/aging-state-prison-population-1993-2013.

72 Eric Finley, "Is Death by Incarceration the New Normal for Aging Prisoners?" Prison Journalism Project, January 31 2023, prisonjournalismproject.org/2023/01/10/is-death-by-incarceration-the-new-normal-for-aging-prisoners.

73 Carson and Sabol, "Aging of the State Prison Population."

74 Nazish Dholakia, "Women's Incarceration Rates Are Skyrocketing. These Advocates Are Trying to Change That," Vera Institute of Justice, May 17, 2021, https://www.vera.org/news/womens-incarceration-rates-are-skyrocketing.

75 Niki Monazzam and Kristen M. Budd, "Incarcerated Women and Girls," Sentencing Project, April 3, 2023, https://www.sentencingproject.org/fact-sheet/incarcerated-women-and-girls.

76 Ayelet Waldman and Robin Levi, eds., *Inside This Place, Not of It* (San Francisco: McSweeney's, 2011), 172.

77 Joseph Shapiro, Jessica Pupovac, and Kari Lyderson, "In Prison, Discipline Comes Down Hardest on Women," NPR, October 15, 2018, https://www.npr.org/2018/10/15/647874342/in-prison-discipline-comes-down-hardest-on-women.

78 "The Unequal Price of Periods: Menstrual Equity in Prison," American Civil Liberties Union, 2019, https://www.aclu.org/wp-content/uploads/legal-documents/111219-sj-periodequity.pdf.

79 "Unequal Price of Periods."

80 Lauren Shaw, "Bloody Hell: How Insufficient Access to Menstrual Hygiene Products Creates Inhumane Conditions for Incarcerated Women," *Texas A&M Law Review* 6, no. 2 (2019), https://doi.org/10.37419/LR.V6.I2.5.

81 Jocelyn Samuels, "Investigation of the Julia Tutwiler Prison for Women and Notice of Expanded Investigation," findings letter, Civil Rights Division, US Department of Justice, January 17, 2014, https://www.justice.gov/sites/default/files/crt/legacy/2014/01/23/tutwiler_findings_1-17-14.pdf.

82 Katie McDonough, "CeCe McDonald on Her Time in Prison: 'I Felt Like They Wanted Me to Hate Myself as a Trans Woman,'" *Salon*, January 19, 2014, www.salon.com/2014/01/19/cece_mcdonald_on_her_time_in_prison_i_felt_like_they_wanted_me_to_hate_myself_as_a_trans_woman.

83 Jason Lydon et al., "Coming Out of Concrete Closets: A Report on Black and Pink's National LGBTQ Prisoner Survey," *Black and Pink*, October 21, 2015, www.blackandpink.org/wp-content/uploads/2020/03/Coming-Out-of-Concrete-Closets-incorcporated-Executive-summary102115.pdf.

84 Aviva Stahl, "The Shocking, Painful Trauma of Being a Trans Prisoner in Solitary Confinement," *Vice*, January 22, 2016, www.vice.com/en/article/qkgq97/the-shocking-painful-trauma-of-being-a-trans-prisoner-in-solitary-confinement.

85 Lydon et al., "Coming Out of Concrete Closets."

86 Lydon et al., "Coming Out of Concrete Closets."

87 Rebecca Vallas, "Disabled behind Bars," Center for American Progress, July 18, 2016, https://www.americanprogress.org/article/disabled-behind-bars.

88   Vallas, "Disabled behind Bars."
89   Maruschak, Bronson, and Alper, "Disabilities Reported by Prisoners."
90   "HB 2002, Testimony in Support of Converting Mandatory Minimum Sentences for
        Specified Felonies Other than Murder to Presumptive Sentences," Disability Rights
        Oregon, February 25, 2021, https://olis.oregonlegislature.gov/liz/2021R1/Downloads/
        PublicTestimonyDocument/7870.
91   Vallas, "Disabled behind Bars."
92   Vallas, "Disabled behind Bars."
93   Jason Schnittker, Michael Massoglia, and Christopher Uggen, "Out and Down:
        Incarceration and Psychiatric Disorders," Journal of Health and Social Behavior 53,
        no. 4: 448–64, https://doi.org/10.1177/0022146512453928.
94   Elizabeth Weill-Greenberg, "Disabled and Abandoned in New York State Prisons,"
        The Nation, October 25, 2021, www.thenation.com/article/society/prisons-
        disability-new-york.
95   Maruschak, Bronson, and Alper, "Disabilities Reported by Prisoners."
96   Jamelia Morgan, "Caged In: The Devastating Harms of Solitary Confinement on
        Prisoners with Physical Disabilities," Buffalo Human Rights Law Review 24 (2018),
        https://digitalcommons.law.buffalo.edu/cgi/viewcontent.cgi?article=1214&context=
        bhrlr.
97   Christie Thompson, "Why Many Deaf Prisoners Can't Call Home," Marshall Project,
        September 19, 2017, www.themarshallproject.org/2017/09/19/why-many-deaf-
        prisoners-can-t-call-home.
98   Vallas, "Disabled behind Bars."
99   James Austin, Kelly Dedel Johnson, and Maria Gregoriou, "Juveniles in Adult Prisons
        and Jails: A National Assessment," Bureau of Justice Assistance, US Department of
        Justice, October 2000, https://www.ojp.gov/pdffiles1/bja/182503.pdf.
100   Nick Vadala, "The Pennsylvania 'Kids for Cash' Scandal Explained," Philadelphia
        Inquirer, August 18, 2022, https://www.inquirer.com/news/pennsylvania/
        pa-kids-for-cash-scandal-judges-mark-ciavarella-michael-conahan-20220818.html.
101   Wendy Sawyer, "Youth Confinement: The Whole Pie 2019," Prison Policy Initiative,
        December 19, 2019, www.prisonpolicy.org/reports/youth2019.html.
102   Shannan Wilber, "Lesbian, Gay, Bisexual and Transgender Youth in the Juvenile Justice
        System," Annie E. Casey Foundation, September 28, 2015, https://assets.aecf.org/m/
        resourcedoc/AECF-lesbiangaybisexualandtransgenderyouthinjj-2015.pdf.
103   Josh Rovner, "Too Many Locked Doors: The Scope of Youth Confinement Is Vastly
        Understated," Sentencing Project, March 15, 2022, www.sentencingproject.org/app/
        uploads/2022/10/too-many-locked-doors.pdf.
104   "Kids Deserve Better: Why Juvenile Detention Reform Matters," Annie E. Casey
        Foundation, December 5, 2018, www.aecf.org/blog/kids-deserve-better-why-
        juvenile-detention-reform-matters.
105   Andrea J. Sedlak and Karla S. McPherson, "Survey of Youth in Residential Placement:
        Youth's Needs and Services," Office of Juvenile Justice and Delinquency Prevention
        bulletin, April 2010, https://www.ncjrs.gov/pdffiles1/ojjdp/227728.pdf.
106   Eli Hager, "Many Juvenile Jails Are Now Almost Entirely Filled with Young People of
        Color," Marshall Project, March 8, 2021, www.themarshallproject.org/2021/03/08/
        many-juvenile-jails-are-now-almost-entirely-filled-with-young-people-of-color.
107   Hager, "Many Juvenile Jails."

108   Erik Ortiz and Jonathan Sperling, "Miami Corrections Officer Charged in Teen's Death Used Bribery System, Indictment Says," NBC News, April 30, 2018, www.nbcnews.com/news/us-news/miami-corrections-officer-charged-teen-s-death-used-bribery-system-n870196.

109   Charles Puzzanchera, Sarah Hockenberry, and Melissa Sickmund, "Youth and the Juvenile Justice System: 2022 National Report," National Center for Juvenile Justice, December 2022, https://ojjdp.ojp.gov/publications/2022-national-report.pdf.

110   Peter A. Schey and Carlos R. Holguin, "Urgent Petition to United Nations Working Group on Arbitrary Detention," Disability Rights Legal Center, March 20, 2012, https://www.scribd.com/document/87095186/Petition-to-UN-Working-Group-on-Arbitrary-Detention.

111   David Reutter, "California Prisoners Unite in Hunger Strike to Protest SHU," *Prison Legal News*, March 7, 2017, www.prisonlegalnews.org/news/2016/mar/7/california-prisoners-unite-in-hunger-strike-protest-shu.

112   Josh Harkinson and Maggie Caldwell, "50 Days without Food: The California Prison Hunger Strike Explained," *Mother Jones*, August 27, 2013, www.motherjones.com/politics/2013/08/50-days-california-prisons-hunger-strike-explainer.

113   "Landmark Agreement Ends Indeterminate Long-Term Solitary Confinement in California," Center for Constitutional Rights, September 1, 2015, ccrjustice.org/home/press-center/press-releases/landmark-agreement-ends-indeterminate-long-term-solitary.

114   Nermeen Shaikh et al., "California Prisoners Challenge Solitary, Jail Conditions with Largest Hunger Strike in State History," *Democracy Now!*, transcript, July 17, 2013, https://www.democracynow.org/2013/7/17/california_prisoners_challenge_solitary_jail_conditions.

115   Dan Brent, "Man Fights for Justice inside Alabama Prison" *People's World*, December 1, 2014, peoplesworld.org/article/man-fights-for-justice-inside-alabama-prison.

116   Angelo, *Prisoners' Inventions* (Chicago: Half Letter Press, 2020).

117   Joseph Darius Jaafari, "The Underground Art of Prison Tattoos," *Marshall Project*, June 7, 2019, www.themarshallproject.org/2019/06/07/the-underground-art-of-prison-tattoos.

118   Nigel Poor and Earlonne Woods, *This Is Ear Hustle: Unflinching Stories of Everyday Prison Life* (New York: Crown, 2022).

119   Zara Stone, "Beauty Behind Bars: Why Makeup Matters for Prisoners," CNN, November 2, 2021, https://www.cnn.com/style/article/prisoners-makeup-pandemic.

120   Angelo, *Prisoners' Inventions*.

121   Harlin Pierce, "When the Prison Banned Board Games, We Played Chess in Our Minds," *Life Inside* (blog), Marshall Project, February 12, 2021, www.themarshallproject.org/2021/02/11/when-the-prison-banned-board-games-we-played-chess-in-our-minds.

122   Emily Nonko, "San Quentin's Breakthrough Prison Newsroom," *Politico*, June 25, 2020, www.politico.com/news/magazine/2020/06/25/criminal-justice-prison-conditions-san-quentin-media-335709.

123   Olivia Heffernan, "Why Prison Journalism Matters," *Jacobin*, April 29, 2022, https://jacobin.com/2022/04/prison-journalism-newspapers-mass-incarceration-criminal-justice

124 Emily D. Buehler, "Justice Expenditure and Employment in the United States, 2017," Bureau of Justice Statistics, US Department of Justice, July 2021, https://bjs.ojp.gov/sites/g/files/xyckuh236/files/media/document/jeeus17.pdf; Tracey Kyckelhahn, "Justice Expenditure and Employment in the United States 1982–2007," Bureau of Justice Statistics, US Department of Justice, December 2011, https://www.prisonlegalnews.org/media/publications/bjs_justice_fy_1982-2007_expenditures_and_employment_statistics_2011.pdf

125 Kristen M. Budd and Niki Monazzam, "Private Prisons in the United States," Sentencing Project, June 15, 2023, https://www.sentencingproject.org/reports/private-prisons-in-the-united-states.

126 Budd and Monazzam, "Private Prisons."

127 "Aramark," Investigate, a Project of the American Friends Service Committee, March 18, 2021, https://investigate.afsc.org/company/aramark.

128 Keri Blakinger, "Ewwwww, What Is That?," Marshall Project, May 11, 2020, www.themarshallproject.org/2020/05/11/ewwwww-what-is-that.

129 "Aramark."

130 Leslie Soble, Kathryn Stroud, and Marika Weinstein, "Eating behind Bars: Ending the Hidden Punishment of Food in Prison," Impact Justice, 2020, impactjustice.org/impact/food-in-prison/#report.

131 Peter Wagner and Wanda Bertram, "State of Phone Justice 2022: The Problem, the Progress, and What's Next," Prison Policy Initiative, December 2022, www.prisonpolicy.org/phones/state_of_phone_justice_2022.html.

132 Victoria Law, "How a Group of Imprisoned Hackers Introduced JPay to the World," Wired, July 27, 2018, www.wired.com/story/how-a-group-of-imprisoned-hackers-introduced-jpay-to-the-world.

133 Brian Dolinar, "Profiting Off Mass Incarceration: Detroit Pistons Owner Buys Private Prison Phone Company," Prison Legal News, October 10, 2017, www.prisonlegalnews.org/news/2017/oct/10/profiting-mass-incarceration-detroit-pistons-owner-buys-private-prison-phone-company.

134 Tommaso Bardelli, Ruqaiyah Zarook, and Derick McCarthy, "How Corporations Turned Prison Tablets into a Predatory Scheme," Dissent, March 7, 2022, www.dissentmagazine.org/online_articles/corporations-prison-tablets-predatory-scheme.

135 Jason Szep et al., "U.S. Jails Are Outsourcing Medical Care—and the Death Toll Is Rising," Reuters, October 26, 2020, https://www.reuters.com/article/us-usa-jails-privatization-special-repor/special-report-u-s-jails-are-outsourcing-medical-care-and-the-death-toll-is-rising-idUSKBN27B1DH.

136 C.J. Ciaramella, "Federal Judge Rules Gruesome Medical Neglect in Arizona Prisons Violates Eighth Amendment," Reason, July 1, 2022, https://reason.com/2022/07/01/federal-judge-rules-gruesome-medical-neglect-in-arizona-prisons-violates-eighth-amendment.

137 Walter Jordan, "2262 Notice of Impending Death Filed by Non Party W Jordan," Marshall Project, February 20, 2018, https://www.themarshallproject.org/documents/4382337-2262-Notice-of-Impending-Death-Filed-by-Non.

138 "Captive Labor: Exploitation of Incarcerated Workers," ACLU and GHRC Research Report, American Civil Liberties Union and the University of Chicago Law School Global Human Rights Clinic, 2022, https://www.aclu.org/report/captive-labor-exploitation-incarcerated-workers.

139   "Captive Labor."

140   "The Prison Industrial Complex: Mapping Private Sector Players," Worth Rises, April 2019, https://worthrises.org/theprisonindustry2019.

141   Wagner and Rabuy, "Following the Money."

142   Wagner and Rabuy, "Following the Money."

143   Stephen Raher, "The Multi-million Dollar Market of Sending Money to an Incarcerated Loved One," Prison Policy Initiative, January 18, 2017, www.prisonpolicy.org/blog/2017/01/18/money-transfer.

144   Wendy Sawyer, "How Much Do Incarcerated People Earn in Each State?" Prison Policy Initiative, April 10, 2017, www.prisonpolicy.org/blog/2017/04/10/wages.

145   Kaia Hubbard, "10 States with the Largest Drops in Prison Population," *US News and World Report*, January 25, 2021.

146   Kassandra Frederique, presentation for Clergy for a New Drug Policy, March 10, 2020.

147   Michelle Alexander, *The New Jim Crow: Mass Incarceration in the Age of Colorblindness* (New York: The New Press, 2020).

148   Sam Levine, "How Republicans Gutted the Biggest Voting Rights Victory in Recent History," *Guardian*, August 6, 2020, https://www.theguardian.com/us-news/2020/aug/06/republicans-florida-amendment-4-voting-rights.

149   Mariame Kaba, "So You're Thinking about Becoming an Abolitionist," *LEVEL*, October 30, 2020, level.medium.com/so-youre-thinking-about-becoming-an-abolitionist-a436f8e31894.

150   Qu'eed Batts, Avron Holland, David Lee, and Nyako Pippen, *Weology: Transformative Justice in Practice* (Philadelphia: LifeLines, 2021), 15.

151   Fania Davis, *The Little Book of Race and Restorative Justice: Black Lives, Healing and US Social Transformation* (New York: Good Books, 2019).

Colophon

The cover is set in Carrie, designed by Tré Seals of Vocal Type Company. The section titles are set in Martin, also designed by Tré Seals. Our titles are set in Program, a typeface designed by Zuzana Licko. Our body is set in Freight, designed by Joshua Darden. Our captions are set in Halyard, also designed by Joshua Darden.

Acknowledgments

I am grateful for the love and support I have received over the years from my family, who were my rock for more than three decades of life as a fugitive and a prisoner. My mother, the late Barbara Kilgore, my life partner, Terri Barnes, our two sons, Lewis and Lonnie, and their grandmother Pat Barnes-McConnell repeatedly taught me the meaning of unconditional love, deep understanding, and sharing the treasures of life. I thank my comrades in South Africa, especially Laura Czerniewicz, Rick DeSatge, Moses Cloete, and Ighsaan Schroeder, and my Australian friends, Stephen Morrow, Roger and Kordula Dunscombe, and Margaret Waller, who kept me in books while I was in prison and shared their wisdom and generous hearts over the years. Lastly I am grateful to all those who helped me find a home in Champaign-Urbana, Illinois, especially those I worked with in FirstFollowers: Marlon Mitchell, James "Tygar" Corbin, Emmett Sanders, and Tamika Davis-Nunez.

—JAMES

This book wouldn't exist without James taking a chance on a cold email and the stranger behind it. Thanks for your faith and trust in me.

As you could imagine, this book was one of the most emotionally taxing projects I've had the honor to undertake. I don't know if I would have finished it without my life partner, Alex Tait. The reality of being a creative with mental illnesses is that your work and life is a group effort of people that make you tea and give you acorns in the midst of an apocalypse and respond to your all caps texts with equal vigor at all hours of the day. Friends, thank you. You keep me alive. Thanks in particular to Frances Van Ganson, who is the best bulwark for bouncing things off of.

Thank you to my family for building my bones. And finally, thank you immensely to everyone who tries and dares to hope in their corners of the world. I am forever grateful to you.

—VIC

About the Creators

JAMES KILGORE is a researcher and activist based in Urbana, Illinois. He is the author of six books, including the National Book Foundation Award–winning *A People's Guide to Mass Incarceration*. He drafted four of those volumes during his six and a half years in California prisons. He is the Building Community Power Fellow at Community Justice Exchange and the director of advocacy and outreach for FirstFollowers Reentry Program in Champaign, Illinois.

VIC LIU is an artist and author who uses design to communicate complex information with empathy. Most recently, Vic published the expanded version of her visually designed masturbation sex-ed book, *Bang! Masturbation for All Genders and Abilities*.

About PM Press

PM Press is an independent, radical publisher of critically necessary books for our tumultuous times. Our aim is to deliver bold political ideas and vital stories to all walks of life and arm the dreamers to demand the impossible. Founded in 2007 by a small group of people with decades of publishing, media, and organizing experience, we have sold millions of copies of our books, most often one at a time, face to face. We're old enough to know what we're doing and young enough to know what's at stake. Join us to create a better world.

PM Press
PO Box 23912
Oakland CA 94623
510-703-0327
www.pmpress.org

PM Press in Europe
europe@pmpress.org
www.pmpress.org.uk

Friends of PM Press

These are indisputably momentous times—the financial system is melting down globally and the Empire is stumbling. Now more than ever there is a vital need for radical ideas. In the many years since its founding—and on a mere shoestring—PM Press has risen to the formidable challenge of publishing and distributing knowledge and entertainment for the struggles ahead. With hundreds of releases to date, we have published an impressive and stimulating array of literature, art, music, politics, and culture. Using every available medium, we've succeeded in connecting those hungry for ideas and information to those putting them into practice.

Friends of PM allows you to directly help impact, amplify, and revitalize the discourse and actions of radical writers, filmmakers, and artists. It provides us with a stable foundation from which we can build upon our early successes and provides a much-needed subsidy for the materials that can't necessarily pay their own way. You can help make that happen—and receive every new title automatically delivered to your door once a month—by joining as a Friend of PM Press. And, we'll throw in a free T-shirt when you sign up.

Here are your options:

- O *$30 a month* Get all books and pamphlets plus 50% discount on all webstore purchases
- O *$40 a month* Get all PM Press releases (including CDs and DVDs) plus 50% discount on all webstore purchases
- O *$100 a month* Superstar—Everything plus PM merchandise, free downloads, and 50% discount on all webstore purchases

For those who can't afford $30 or more a month, we have *Sustainer Rates* at $15, $10, and $5. Sustainers get a free PM Press T-shirt and a 50% discount on all purchases from our website.

Your Visa or Mastercard will be billed once a month, until you tell us to stop. Or until our efforts succeed in bringing the revolution around. Or the financial meltdown of Capital makes plastic redundant. Whichever comes first.

A People's Guide to Abolition and Disability Justice

Katie Tastrom

ISBN: 979-8-88744-040-8 • $19.95
5 x 8 • 256 pages

Disability justice and prison abolition are two increasingly popular theories that overlap but whose intersection has rarely been explored in depth.

A People's Guide to Abolition and Disability Justice explains the history and theories behind abolition and disability justice in a way that is easy to understand for those new to these concepts yet also gives insights that will be useful to seasoned activists. The book uses extensive research and professional and lived experience to illuminate the way the State uses disability and its power to disable to incarcerate multiply marginalized disabled people, especially those who are queer, trans, Black, or Indigenous.

Because disabled people are much more likely than nondisabled people to be locked up in prisons, jails, and other sites of incarceration, abolitionists and others critical of carceral systems must incorporate a disability justice perspective into our work. *A People's Guide to Abolition and Disability Justice* gives personal and policy examples of how and why disabled people are disproportionately caught up in the carceral net, and how we can use this information to work toward prison and police abolition more effectively. This book includes practical tools and strategies that will be useful for anyone who cares about disability justice or abolition and explains why we can't have one without the other.

> "Reminding us that abolition and disability justice must be, on a molecular level, grown together, Katie Tastrom offers a manifesto, which is also to say an atlas that leads us deeper into this analysis. Pushing against a world where harms lived by some are reproduced under the promise of safety for others, Tastrom insists that we must dream of more. Working from personal experience and a wide genealogy of abolitionist crip thought, this book is a necessary contribution to our collective study."
> —Eric A. Stanley, *author of* Atmospheres of Violence: Structuring Antagonism and the Trans/Queer Ungovernable

"An essential movement tool. Tastrom convincingly shows that police and prison abolition and disability justice are core strategies for liberation and that we can't win one without the other."
—ALEX VITALE, author of *The End of Policing*

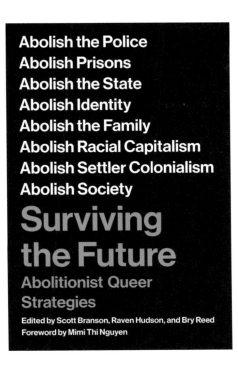

Abolish the Police
Abolish Prisons
Abolish the State
Abolish Identity
Abolish the Family
Abolish Racial Capitalism
Abolish Settler Colonialism
Abolish Society

Surviving the Future
Abolitionist Queer Strategies

Edited by Scott Branson, Raven Hudson, and Bry Reed
Foreword by Mimi Thi Nguyen

Surviving the Future
Abolitionist Queer Strategies

Edited by Scott Branson, Raven Hudson, and Bry Reed • Foreword by Mimi Thi Nguyen

ISBN: 978-1-62963-971-0 • $22.95
6 x 9 • 328 pages

Surviving the Future is a collection of the most current ideas in radical queer movement work and revolutionary queer theory. Beset by a new pandemic, fanning the flames of global uprising, these queers cast off progressive narratives of liberal hope while building mutual networks of rebellion and care. These essays propose a militant strategy of queer survival in an ever-precarious future. Starting from a position of abolition—of prisons, police, the State, identity, and racist cisheteronormative society—this collection refuses the bribes of inclusion in a system built on our expendability. Though the mainstream media saturates us with the boring norms of queer representation (with a recent focus on trans visibility), the writers in this book ditch false hope to imagine collective visions of liberation that tell different stories, build alternate worlds, and refuse the legacies of racial capitalism, anti-Blackness, and settler colonialism. The work curated in this book spans Black queer life in the time of COVID-19 and uprising, assimilation and pinkwashing settler colonial projects, subversive and deviant forms of representation, building anarchist trans/queer infrastructures, and more. Contributors include Che Gossett, Yasmin Nair, Mattilda Bernstein Sycamore, Adrian Shanker, Kitty Stryker, Toshio Meronek, and more.

> "Surviving the Future *is a testament that otherwise worlds are not only possible, our people are making them right now—and they are queering how we get there through organizing and intellectual work. Now is the perfect time to interrogate how we are with each other and the land we inhabit. This collection gives us ample room to do just that in a moment of mass uprisings led by everyday people demanding safety without policing, prisons and other forms of punishment.*"
> —*Charlene A. Carruthers, author of* Unapologetic: A Black, Queer, and Feminist Mandate for Radical Movements

Look for Me in the Whirlwind
From the Panther 21 to 21st-Century Revolutions

Sekou Odinga, Dhoruba Bin Wahad, Jamal Joseph • Edited by dequi kioni-sadiki and Matt Meyer

ISBN: 978-1-62963-389-3 • $26.95
6 x 9 • 648 pages

Amid music festivals and moon landings, the tumultuous year of 1969 included an infamous case in the annals of criminal justice and Black liberation: the New York City Black Panther 21. Though some among the group had hardly even met one another, the 21 were rounded up by the FBI and New York Police Department in an attempt to disrupt and destroy the organization that was attracting young people around the world. Involving charges of conspiracy to commit violent acts, the Panther 21 trial—the longest and most expensive in New York history—revealed the illegal government activities which led to exile, imprisonment on false charges, and assassination of Black liberation leaders. Solidarity for the 21 also extended well beyond "movement" circles and included mainstream publication of their collective autobiography, *Look for Me in the Whirlwind*, which is reprinted here for the first time.

Look for Me in the Whirlwind contains the entire original manuscript, and includes new commentary from surviving members of the 21: Sekou Odinga, Dhoruba Bin Wahad, Jamal Joseph, and Shaba Om. Still-imprisoned Sundiata Acoli, Imam Jamil Al-Amin, and Mumia Abu-Jamal contribute new essays. Never or rarely seen poetry and prose from Afeni Shakur, Kuwasi Balagoon, Ali Bey Hassan, and Michael "Cetewayo" Tabor is included. Early Panther leader and jazz master Bilal Sunni-Ali adds a historical essay and lyrics from his composition "Look for Me in the Whirlwind," and coeditors kioni-sadiki and Meyer and Panther rank-and-file member Cyril "Bullwhip" Innis Jr. help bring the story up to date.

At a moment when the Movement for Black Lives recites the affirmation that "it is our duty to win," penned by Black Liberation Army (BLA) militant Assata Shakur, those who made up the BLA and worked alongside of Assata are largely unknown. This book—with archival photos from David Fenton, Stephen Shames, and the private collections of the authors—provides essential parts of a hidden and missing-in-action history. Going well beyond the familiar and mythologized nostalgic Panther narrative, *From the Panther 21 to 21st-Century Revolutions* explains how and why the Panther legacy is still relevant and vital today.

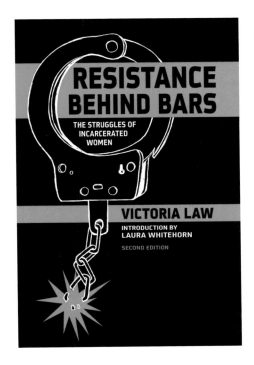

Resistance Behind Bars
The Struggles of Incarcerated Women, 2nd Edition

Victoria Law
Introduction by Laura Whitehorn

ISBN: 978-1-60486-583-7 • $20.00
6 x 9 • 320 pages

In 1974, women imprisoned at New York's maximum-security prison at Bedford Hills staged what is known as the August Rebellion. Protesting the brutal beating of a fellow prisoner, the women fought off guards, holding seven of them hostage, and took over sections of the prison.

While many have heard of the 1971 Attica prison uprising, the August Rebellion remains relatively unknown even in activist circles. *Resistance Behind Bars* is determined to challenge and change such oversights. As it examines daily struggles against appalling prison conditions and injustices, *Resistance* documents both collective organizing and individual resistance among women incarcerated in the US. Emphasizing women's agency in resisting the conditions of their confinement through forming peer education groups, clandestinely arranging ways for children to visit mothers in distant prisons and raising public awareness about their lives, *Resistance* seeks to spark further discussion and research into the lives of incarcerated women and galvanize much-needed outside support for their struggles.

This updated and revised edition of the 2009 PASS Award–winning book includes a new chapter about transgender, transsexual, intersex, and gender-variant people in prison.

> "Victoria Law's eight years of research and writing, inspired by her unflinching commitment to listen to and support women prisoners, has resulted in an illuminating effort to document the dynamic resistance of incarcerated women in the United States."
> —Roxanne Dunbar-Ortiz

The Real Cost of Prisons Comix

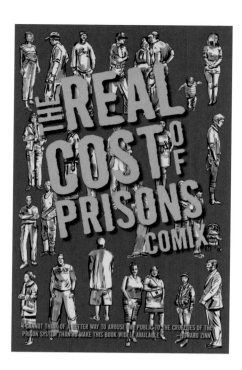

Edited by Lois Ahrens
Written by Ellen Miller-Mack,
Craig Gilmore, Lois Ahrens, Susan
Willmarth, and Kevin Pyle
Illustrated by Kevin Pyle, Sabrina
Jones, and Susan Willmarth
Introduction by Craig Gilmore and
Ruth Wilson Gilmore
ISBN: 978-1-60486-034-4 • $16.95
7 x 10 • 104 pages

Winner of the 2008 PASS Award (Prevention for
a Safer Society) from the National Council on
Crime and Delinquency

One out of every hundred adults in the US is in prison. This book provides a crash course in what drives mass incarceration, the human and community costs, and how to stop the numbers from going even higher. Collected in this volume are the three comic books published by the Real Cost of Prisons Project. The stories and statistical information in each comic book are thoroughly researched and documented.

Prison Town: Paying the Price tells the story of how the financing and site locations of prisons affects the people of rural communities in which prison are built. It also tells the story of how mass incarceration affects people of urban communities where the majority of incarcerated people come from.

Prisoners of the War on Drugs includes the history of the war on drugs, mandatory minimums, how racism creates harsher sentences for people of color, how the war on drugs works against women, three strikes laws, obstacles to coming home after incarceration, and how mass incarceration destabilizes neighborhoods.

Prisoners of a Hard Life: Women and Their Children includes stories about women trapped by mandatory sentencing and the "costs" of incarceration for women and their families.

The book includes a chapter with descriptions of how the comix have been put to use in the work of organizers and activists in prison and in the "free world" by ESL teachers, high school teachers, college professors, students, and health care providers throughout the country. The demand for the comix is constant and the ways in which they are being used are inspiring.